我的家乡中国陕西省，就位于古丝绸之路的起点。站在这里，回顾历史，我仿佛听到了山间回荡的声声驼铃，看到了大漠飘飞的袅袅孤烟。这一切，让我感到十分的亲切。

——习近平

My home town is in Shaanxi, which is the starting point of the ancient Silk Road. Standing on this land and reviewing history, I seem to hear camel bells echoing in valleys, and see smoke curling upward above the great desert. All these are fairly familiar to me.

—Xi Jinping

中华根脉
文化陕西

Zhonghua
Genmai
Wenhua
Shaanxi

2024
中国陕西

2024 CHINA SHAANXI

陕西省人民政府新闻办公室 编

Information Office of Shaanxi
Provincial People's
Government

陕西新华出版
陕西人民出版社

引言
Introduction

了解中国从陕西开始

To Learn about China, One must Begin from Shaanxi

陕西，地处中国地理版图的几何中心，承东启西、连接南北，区位独特，是中华民族和华夏文化的重要发祥地之一，也是古丝绸之路的东方起点，拥有黄帝陵、兵马俑、延安宝塔山、秦岭、华山等中华文明、中国革命、中华地理的精神标识和自然标识。陕西，自古以来就是中国重要的对外开放门户，"一带一路"使它成为向西开放的前沿，如今，它正在焕发着高质量发展的蓬勃生机。

这里，有中华民族的辉煌篇章和深刻印记。周、秦、汉、唐等14个王朝在此建都，留下了近5万处

Situated in the geographical center of China's territory, Shaanxi enjoys a unique location by connecting the south and north of China and linking the east and west of the country. As an important cradle of the Chinese nation and culture, Shaanxi boasts spiritual markers and natural symbols of the Chinese civilization, Chinese revolution and Chinese geography, including the Mausoleum of the Yellow Emperor, the Terracotta Warriors and Horses, Yan'an Pagoda, the Qinling Mountain Range, and Mount Hua. Shaanxi has been an important gateway to the outside world since ancient times. With the implementation of the Belt & Road Initiative, Shaanxi has become the forefront in opening to the west, and is booming with great vitality in high-quality development.

Shaanxi has witnessed the glorious history and profound imprints of the Chinese nation. 14 dynasties, including Zhou, Qin, Han, and Tang, established their capitals in Shaanxi, leaving it the name of "natural historical museum" with almost 50,000 cultural relics sites

文物遗址、770多万件馆藏文物，它是"天然历史博物馆"，诉说着东方文明古国的恒久魅力。

这里，有中国共产党的成功真谛和不变初心。延安、照金等红色基因薪火相传，巍巍宝塔熠熠生辉，一直见证着中国共产党人的伟大奋斗；延安精神历久弥新，激励着一代又一代人砥砺前行。

这里，有当代中国的崭新画卷和精彩故事。党的十八大以来，陕西深度融入共建"一带一路"大格局，着力打造内陆改革开放高地，秦创原成为陕西创新驱动的新引擎，大型运输机、新能源汽车、闪存芯片、高端液晶面板等成为"陕西智造"的新名片。秦腔、华阴老腔、陕北民歌、西安鼓乐等依然高亢嘹亮，历史与现代在这里交相辉映，传统与时尚在这里完美融合。

新时代的陕西，将以习近平新时代中国特色社会主义思想为指

and over 7.7 million collections, showing the world the enduring charm of ancient Eastern civilization.

Shaanxi is bestowed with the true essence of success and unchanged original aspiration of the Communist Party of China. The red revolutionary spirit of Yan'an and Zhaojin is passing down from one generation to the next, and the towering Yan'an Pogada has been witnessing the great struggle of the Communist Party of China. Yan'an Spirit is conveying new interpretations and inspiring generations of Chinese people to forge ahead.

Shaanxi is unfolding the magnificent progress and inspiring events of China in the contemporary times. Since the 18th National Congress of the CPC, Shaanxi has been vigorously involved in the great framework of the Belt & Road Initiative and making unremitting efforts in building a new highland for inland reform and opening up. Qinchuangyuan has become a new driving force for Shaanxi's innovative development. Large transport aircraft, new energy vehicles, flash memory chips, high-end LCD panels, etc. have become new business cards of "Shaanxi Intelligent Manufacturing". Shaanxi Opera, Huayin Laoqiang Opera, Northern Shaanxi Ballads, and Xi'an Drum Music are still yielding brilliance and charm, showing perfect complementation of history and modernity, and integration of tradition and fashion.

In the new era, following the guidance of Xi Jinping Thought on Socialism with Chinese Characteristics for a New Era, Shaanxi will fully implement the guiding

导，全面贯彻落实党的二十大精神，坚持稳中求进工作总基调，完整、准确、全面贯彻新发展理念，着力推动高质量发展，更好服务和融入新发展格局，奋力谱写中国式现代化建设的陕西新篇章。

来到陕西，可触摸中华民族生生不息的根脉，可尽览中华人文多姿多彩的风情，可感知中国变革行稳致远的律动。了解中国，从陕西开始！

principles of the Party's 20th National Congress, act on the general principle of pursuing progress while ensuring stability, apply the new development philosophy in full, in the right way, and in all fields of endeavor, and focus on promoting high-quality development, so as to better serve and integrate into the new development paradigm, and strive to write Shaanxi's chapter in China's modernization drive.

In Shaanxi, you can touch the roots and feel the pulse of the vigorous Chinese nation, appreciate the colorful charm of Chinese culture, and experience the steady and profound rhythm of reform in China. To learn about China, one must begin from Shaanxi!

秦岭终南山

目录
Contents

第一篇
人杰地灵，底蕴深厚
长安回望绣成堆

Chapter One
Inspiring Place with Outstanding People and Profound Heritage
Viewed from Chang'an, Mount Li Looks like a Piece of Embroidery

自然环境
Natural Environment
002

历史文化
History and Culture
010

旅游胜地
Tourism Attractions
022

千年古都，常来长安——大唐不夜城
The Great Tang All Day Mall: Welcome to Chang'an, an Ancient City with Over One Thousand Years of History
036

第二篇
青山绿水，持续发展
林间新绿一重重

Chapter Two
Lush Mountains and Lucid Waters for Sustainable Development
New Green Leaves Throbbing among Branches

国土增绿	生物保护	河流与湿地
Land Greening	Biological Conservation	Rivers and Wetlands
040	044	048

诗经故里——合阳湿地

The Cradle of *The Book of Songs*: Heyang Wetland

052

第三篇
蓬勃生机，开拓进取
晴空一鹤排云上

Chapter Three
Booming with Vitality and Forging Ahead
A Crane Flapping Its Wings to the Clear Sky

发展潜力	特色产业	经济布局
Development Potential	Specialty Industries	Economic Layout
056	064	072

东方宝石——朱鹮

Crested Ibis: Oriental Jewel

078

第四篇
安居乐业，脱贫致富
丰年留客足鸡豚

Chapter Four
Living and Working in Peace, Shaking off Poverty and Getting Rich
Ample Food for Guests in Good Years

便捷出行
Convenient Transportation
082

民生工程
Livelihood Projects
086

乡村振兴
Rural Revitalization
094

秦东沃野，关中粮仓——关中平原
Guanzhong Plain: A Fertile Land in Eastern Shaanxi and the Granary of Guanzhong
100

第五篇
海纳百川，兼容并包
百川衮衮东赴海

Chapter Five
Embracing and All-inclusive
All Rivers Flowing East to the Sea

融入"一带一路"
Response to the "Belt and Road Initiative"
104

成功举行中国—中亚峰会
Successfully Hosting the the China-Central Asia Summit
110

自贸区建设
Free Trade Zone Construction
112

国际交流合作
International Exchange and Cooperation
118

2024 年陕西经济社会发展主要目标
Major Social and Economic Goals of Shaanxi Province in 2024
122

天下黄河一壶收——壶口瀑布
The Magnificent Scenery of the Yellow River: Hukou Waterfall
124

附录
Annex

附录一 三秦城市概览
Annex Ⅰ Overview of Major Cities in Shaanxi Province
129

附录二 2016年以来，陕西入选"全国十大考古新发现"的考古遗址
Annex Ⅱ Shaanxi's Archaeological Sites Listed on China's Annual Top 10 Archaeological Sites Discovered since 2016
134

附录三 巧夺天工的陕西国宝级文物
Annex Ⅲ Shaanxi Cultural Relics with Exquisite Workmanship
138

附录四 陕西第一批"国家级非物质文化遗产"名录
Annex Ⅳ The First Batch of "National Intangible Cultural Heritage" in Shaanxi
140

附录五 陕西特产
Annex Ⅴ Shaanxi Specialties
142

附录六 陕西精华旅游线路
Annex Ⅵ Best Tourist Routes in Shaanxi
146

附录七 陕西小吃
Annex Ⅶ Shaanxi Snacks
148

陕西地理位置优越，地貌丰富多样，资源丰沛，是中华民族及华夏文明的重要发祥地之一，有周、秦、汉、唐等 10 多个政权或朝代在此建都，留下了无数历史文化遗产。黄帝陵、兵马俑、延安宝塔山、秦岭、华山等是中华文明、中国革命、中华地理的精神标识和自然标识，"看五千年中国到陕西"，是人们对陕西悠久历史和厚重文化的形象描述。

Boasting advantageous location, varied landforms, and rich resources, Shaanxi is an important cradle of the Chinese nation and culture. Over 10 powers and dynasties established their capitals in Shaanxi, including the Zhou, the Qin, the Han, and the Tang Dynasties, leaving behind them countless historical and cultural relics. The Mausoleum of the Yellow Emperor, the Terracotta Warriors and Horses, Yan'an Pagoda, the Qinling Mountain Range, and Mount Hua are the spiritual and natural symbols of the Chinese civilization, the Chinese revolution, and the Chinese geography. "Shaanxi is where people can appreciate 5,000-year Chinese history". This is a vivid description of Shaanxi's profound history and culture.

>

Chapter One

第一篇

人杰地灵，底蕴深厚

长安回望绣成堆

Inspiring Place with Outstanding People and Profound Heritage

Viewed from Chang'an, Mount Li Looks like a Piece of Embroidery

自然环境
Natural Environment

地理位置
Geographical Location

陕西位于东经105°29′—111°15′、北纬31°42′—39°35′，地处中国内陆腹地，东邻山西、河南，西连宁夏、甘肃，南抵四川、重庆、湖北，北接内蒙古，是连接

Shaanxi is situated at the hinterland of China at longitude of 105°29′–111°15′ east and latitude of 31°42′–39°35′ north. It neighbors the provinces of Shanxi and Henan to the east, Ningxia Hui Autonomous Region and Gansu Province to the west, Sichuan Province, Chongqing Municipality and Hubei Province to the south, and Inner

秦岭北麓的翠华山景区

中国东、中部和西北、西南的交通枢纽。中国的大地原点就在陕西省泾阳县永乐镇。

陕西下辖西安、宝鸡、咸阳、铜川、渭南、延安、榆林、汉中、安康、商洛10个省辖市和杨凌农业高新技术产业示范区；2023年末，陕西省有常住人口3952万人。

Mongolia Autonomous Region to the north. With convenient transportation links and a strategic location, it serves as a hub which connects eastern and central China with northwestern and southwestern China. The geodetic origin of China is found in Yongle Town, Jingyang County, Shaanxi Province.

Shaanxi has jurisdiction over 10 provincially-governed cities, namely Xi'an, Baoji, Xianyang, Tongchuan, Weinan, Yan'an, Yulin, Hanzhong, Ankang and Shangluo, as well as the Yangling Agricultural High-tech Industries Demonstration Zone. By 2023, Shaanxi Province has a permanent population of 39.52 million.

陕西省行政区划简图

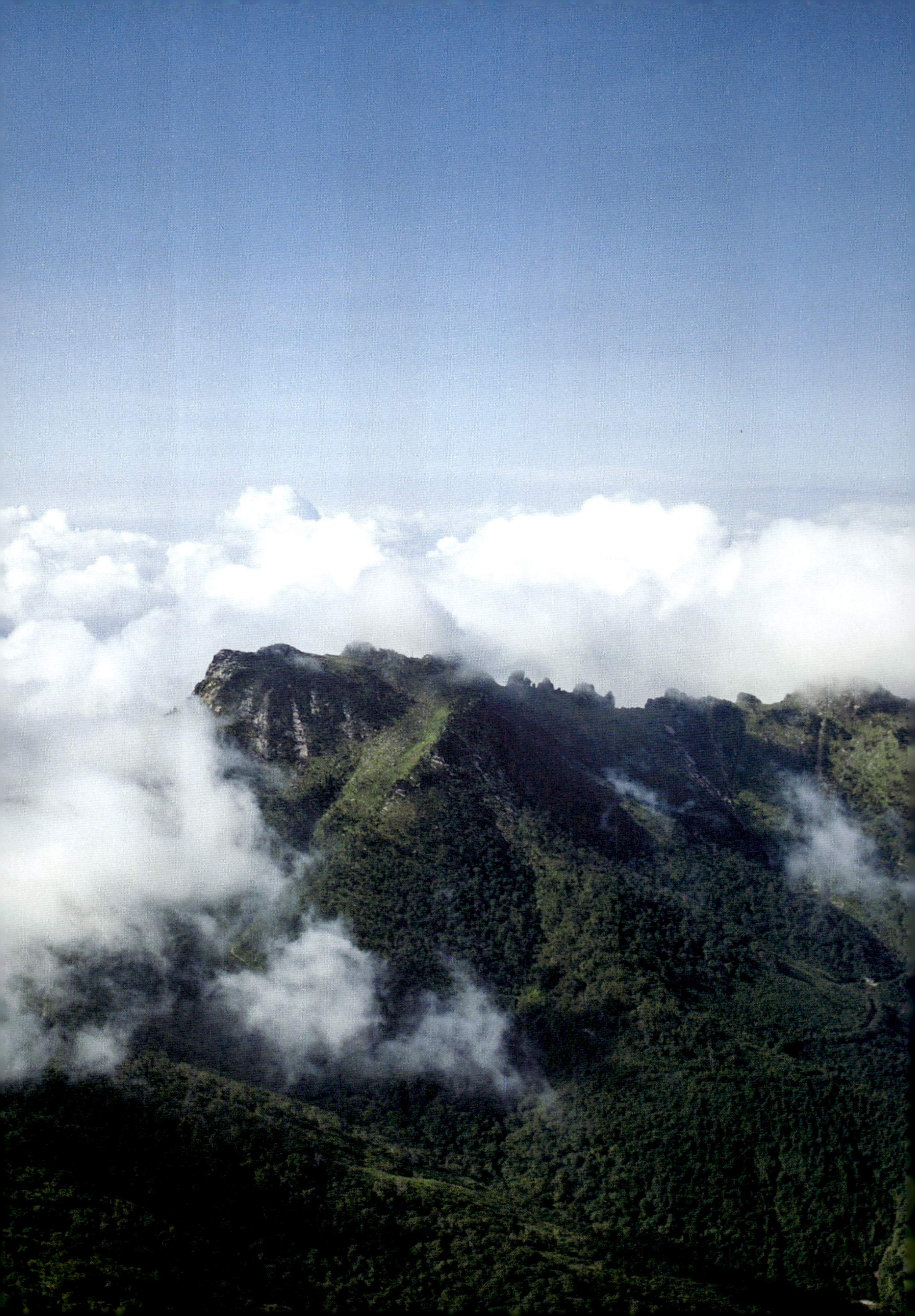

巍巍秦岭

地形地貌
Landform

陕西总面积20.56万平方千米，纵跨长江、黄河两大流域和中温、暖温、亚热三个气候带，自然形成了陕北、关中、陕南三大区域。地域南北狭长，地势南北高、中间

With a total area of 205,600 square kilometers, Shaanxi spans the basins of the Yangtze River and the Yellow River, covering intermediate, warm temperate and subtropical climatic zones. The province consists of three parts: Northern Shaanxi, Guanzhong, and Southern Shaanxi. Topographically, Shaanxi is long and narrow, with higher altitudes in the south and the north and lower elevation in the middle. Within the

西岳华山

低，有高原、山地、平原和盆地等多种地形，因此陕西省各地气候、水文、地貌差异较大，特色鲜明。秦岭全长1600多千米，是中国南北方的分界线。

territory of Shaanxi, there are various landforms, such as plateaus, mountainous regions, plains and basins. Thus, the climate, hydrology and geomorphology vary across the province with distinctive characteristics. The over 1,600 km-long Qinling Mountain Range, is the great provincially-governed between the northern and southern parts of China.

丰沛资源
Rich Resources

陕西是中国的资源大省，已发现矿产138种。陕西矿产资源在全国占据重要位置，岩盐保有资源储量位居全国第一位，石油和天然气位居全国第三位，煤炭、钒矿、水泥用灰岩位居全国第四位，钼矿和磷矿位居全国第七位，金矿位居全国第九位。陕西也因此成为国

Shaanxi is a key province rich in resources in China and 138 types of minerals have been found here. It specifically enjoys an important position in the country in terms of mineral resources, with its rock salt reserve ranking first, reserves of petroleum and natural gas ranking the third, reserves of coal, vanadium and limestone used for cement ranking the fourth, reserves of molybdenum ore and phosphate ranking

靖边煤油气资源综合利用项目生产装置

家西气东输、西电东送、西煤东运的重要能源基地。秦岭有野生种子植物3800余种，约占全国的15%。大熊猫、金丝猴、朱鹮、羚牛等119种濒危野生动物在此生息繁衍。陕南秦巴山区拥有丰富的水资源，开发水力发电潜力巨大，并且是中国南水北调中线工程的水源涵养地。

the seventh, reserve of gold ranking the ninth in China. Therefore, Shaanxi has become an important energy base for the west-to-east transmission of gas, electricity and coal in China. The Qinling Mountain Range is home to over 3,800 wild seed plants, accounting for about 15% of the national total, and 119 endangered wild animals, including the panda, the golden monkey, the crested ibis and the takin. The Qinling-Daba Mountainous Range in Southern Shaanxi is rich in water resources and has enormous potential for exploitation of hydropower. It is also a water source for the South-to-North Water Diversion Project.

历史文化
History and Culture

悠久历史
Long History

中华人文始祖黄帝5000多年前在陕西开创了中华文明，位于黄陵县的黄帝陵和位于宝鸡市的炎帝陵，是中华文明发祥地的重要标志。

Around 5,000 years ago, China's cultural ancestor, the Yellow Emperor, created the Chinese civilization in Shaanxi. The Yellow Emperor Mausoleum in Huangling County and Emperor Yandi's Mausoleum in Baoji City are prominent symbols of the birthplace of Chinese civilization.

Altogether 14 dynasties, including the Western Zhou, the Qin, the Han and the Tang, established their capitals in Shaanxi. The Qin Dynasty is the first unified feudal dynasty with a centralized political system in the history of China. The Western Han Dynasty witnessed the integrated development of the society, the economy and the culture. The Silk Road

陕西历史博物馆秦汉馆

中国历史上有西周、秦、汉、唐等 14 个政权在陕西建都。秦朝是中国第一个中央集权的封建王朝。到西汉时期，社会、经济、文化全面发展，汉唐丝绸之路从陕西发端。唐朝是中国历代最强盛的王朝，都城长安不仅是当时中国政治、经济、文化的中心，更是国际闻名的大都市。

唐代以后，统治中心东移，陕西不再是中国政治、经济的中心，但在中国政治、经济和军事上仍占有重要地位，直到近代，一直是西部重镇。

started from Shaanxi during the Han and the Tang dynasties. The Tang Empire was the most powerful among China's dynasties in history. Chang'an, the capital of Tang, was not only the political, economic and cultural center of China, but also a famous international metropolis.

After the Tang Dynasty, the center of governmental administration moved eastward. Shaanxi was no longer the political and economic center of China. However, Shaanxi still occupied an important position in politics, economy and military of China. Up to modern times, Shaanxi has been considered as a crucial area within western China.

红色文化
Revolutionary Culture

陕西是红色革命沃土，延安是中国革命圣地。从1935年到1948年，延安是中共中央的所在地，是中国人民解放斗争的总后方。毛泽东等老一辈革命家培育形成的延安精神，是中华民族精神宝

Shaanxi is the cradle of revolution, and Yan'an is the sacred land of Chinese revolution. From 1935 to March 1948, Yan'an was the home to the CPC Central Committee and the overall rear base for the Chinese people's struggle

库中的宝贵财富。延安现存革命纪念地400余处，其中宝塔山、凤凰山、杨家岭、枣园、王家坪、陕甘宁边区政府旧址等最为著名。

for liberation. The Yan'an Spirit, nurtured by Mao Zedong and other revolutionary leaders of his generation, is great treasure of the Chinese national spirit. Yan'an is home to over 400 old revolutionary sites, among which the most famous ones are Mount Baota, Mount Fenghuang, Yangjialing, Zaoyuan,

延安宝塔山

鲁迅艺术文学院旧址

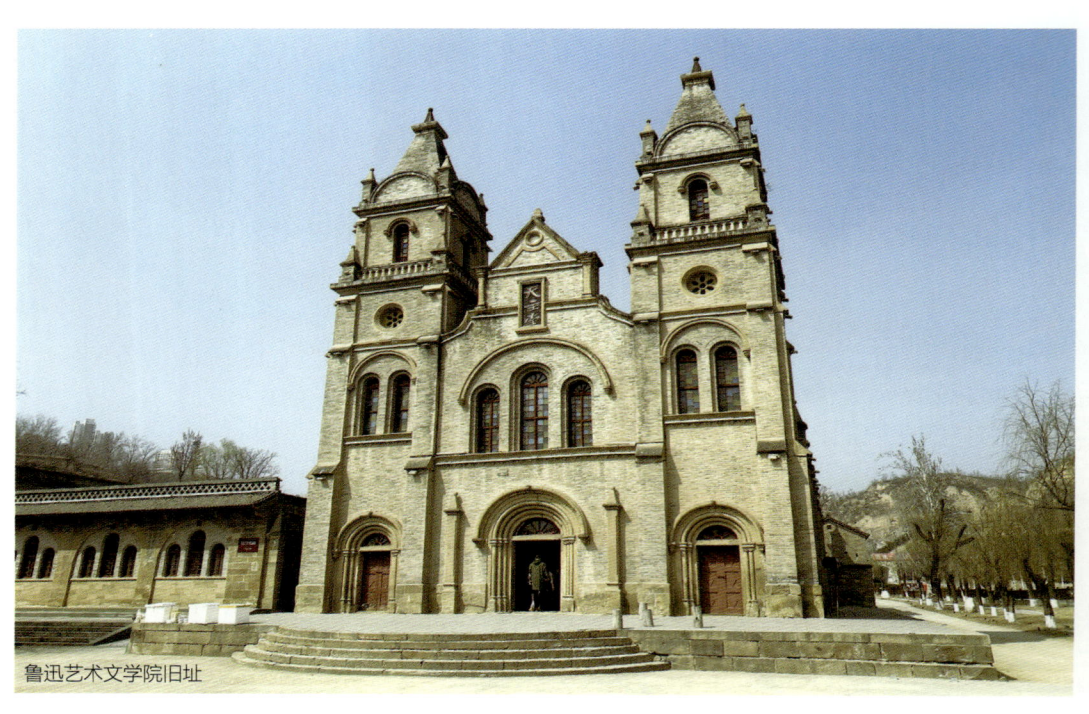

红色小镇照金镇

陕甘边照金革命根据地位于铜川市耀州区。20世纪30年代初,刘志丹、谢子长、习仲勋等老一辈革命家在这里创建了以照金为中心的陕甘边革命根据地。陕甘边照金革命根据地的建立,点燃了西北革命的火种,为后来陕北革命根据地的建立创造了条件,在中国革命史上留下了光辉的一页。

2004年,陕甘边革命根据地照金纪念馆正式开馆,成为全国100个红色旅游经典景区之一。

Wangjiaping and the site of Shaanxi-Gansu-Ningxia Border Government.

The Zhaojin Revolutionary Base in Shaanxi-Gansu Border Region is located at Yaozhou District, Tongchuan City. In the early 1930s, the older generation revolutionary leaders including Liu Zhidan, Xie Zichang and Xi Zhongxun bravely carried out revolutionary activities under extremely arduous conditions. They founded Shaanxi-Gansu Border Region Revolutionary Base with Zhaojin as the center. The establishment of Shaanxi-Gansu Border Region Revolutionary Base kindled the revolution in northwestern China, created conditions for the later Northern Shaanxi Revolutionary Base, and wrote a brilliant chapter in China's revolutionary history.

In 2004, the Memorial Hall of Zhaojin Revolutionary Base in Shaanxi-Gansu Border Region was officially opened. It is one of China's 100 revolutionary scenic spots.

民间文化
Folk Culture

陕西民间艺术丰富多彩，地域特色鲜明。许多项目被列入"国家级非物质文化遗产名录"。户县（今西安市鄠邑区）、安塞（今延安市安塞区）等县区

There are a variety of folk art with outstanding regional features in Shaanxi. Many of them have been included in the list of National Intangible Cultural Heritage. The counties of Huxian（Huyi District, Xi'an）, Ansai （Ansai District,Yan'an）, and other

安塞腰鼓

被文化和旅游部命名为"全国民间绘画之乡";安塞、凤翔、千阳县南寨镇、合阳县甘井镇等被文化和旅游部命名为"中国民间文化艺术之乡";安塞被中国文联、中国曲协评为"中国曲艺之乡",是陕西省唯一的全国文化"五乡"(此前

counties are named as "Hometown of National Folk Painting"; Ansai, Fengxiang counties as well as Nanzhai Township in Qianyang County and Ganjing Township in Heyang County are named as "Hometown of Chinese Folk Art" by Ministry of Culture and Tourism. Ansai County is granted the title "Hometown of Chinese Quyi (ballad-singing and storytelling)" by Chinese Ballad Singers Association and China Federation of Literary and Art Circles. Ansai is the only one in Shaanxi to

安塞被文化和旅游部授予"腰鼓之乡""剪纸之乡""民间绘画之乡""民歌之乡")。目前陕西省入选联合国教科文组织人类非物质文化遗产代表作名录的有西安鼓乐、中国剪纸、中国皮影戏、咸阳茯茶制作技艺四项。

秦腔是中国最具代表性的古老剧种之一,源于陕西、甘肃一带的民间曲调和宋、金、元的铙鼓杂剧,陕甘一带古为秦地,故称其为"秦腔"。又因其以枣木梆子为击节乐器,所以又叫"梆子腔",俗称"乱弹"。

陕北民歌、陕北剪纸具有浓郁的黄土

be named hometown for five sorts of folk art (It was previously granted the honor of hometown of waist drums, paper-cutting, folk painting and folk songs by Ministry of Culture and Tourism). Xi'an Drum Music, Chinese Paper-cutting and Chinese Shadow Puppets have been inscribed in the UNESCO Intangible Cultural Heritage List.

Qin Opera is one of the most representative old operas of China. It originated in the folk tunes and the timbrel opera of the Song, the Jin and the Yuan dynasties along Shaanxi and Gansu. The area around Shaanxi and Gansu was within the territory of the Kingdom of Qin, hence the name Qin Opera. As jujube wood bangzi (slit drum) is used for percussion in the performance, it is also called Bangzi Opera or Luantan (strum) by the locals.

华阴老腔

文化和边塞文化特色；扭秧歌、安塞腰鼓等传统民间艺术也从陕北走向了世界。

华阴老腔曲风高亢豪迈、自在随性，是关中地区的代表性民间文化；社火是关中地区传统的民俗文娱活动；凤翔彩绘泥塑、凤翔木版年画和户县农民画等关中民间艺术体现了丰富多彩的民风民俗。

陕南地区的汉剧为京剧的形成做出过特殊贡献；紫阳民歌是陕南地区传统民歌中最具代表性的曲种。

周至十八会上的"马社火"

Northern Shaanxi Ballads and Northern Shaanxi Paper-cutting enjoy rich Loess and border cultural features. Yangge Performance, Ansai Waist Drum and other traditional folk art spread from Northern Shaanxi to the rest of the world.

Huayin Laoqiang Opera enjoys vigorous, majestic, free and unconstrained features, representative of the folk culture in the Guanzhong Plain. Shehuo (village and township festival parade) is a traditional folk custom and cultural activity in the area. Fengxiang Color-painted Clay Figurines, Fengxiang Xylograph New Year Pictures, Huxian County Peasant Painting, and other folk art in the Guanzhong Plain elaborately and vividly delineate the colorful customs with a plain style.

In Southern Shaanxi, Hanju Opera made special contributions to the formation of the Peking Opera. Ziyang Folk Song is the most representative among traditional folk songs.

现代文化
Modern Culture

随着时代的发展，新兴的文化形态与陕西的古老文化不断交融，创业咖啡街区为陕西创新创业注入了强大动力，成为展示城市新风貌的时尚地标。

With the development of times, new cultural forms continuously integrate with ancient Shaanxi culture. Xi'an Inno Start-up Wonderland infuses new vitality to the city's innovation and development, and has become a beautiful modern landmark for fashion.

Shaanxi Opera House, the first international,

西安蓝海风书店

陕西大剧院是西北地区首个国际化、专业化、综合性的大剧院,也是展示古都文化魅力的重要窗口。

西安音乐厅是西北地区首屈一指的演出场馆,更是享誉古城西安的文化地标。

professional and comprehensive theater in northwestern China, is an important window of Shaanxi to exhibit the cultural charm of its ancient capital.

Xi'an Concert Hall, the No.1 performance venue in northwestern China, is a renowned cultural landmark of the ancient city.

陕西大剧院

旅游胜地
Tourism Attractions

人文之旅
Cultural Tourism

陕西人文旅游资源丰富，有黄帝陵、炎帝陵、秦始皇陵以及汉唐帝陵等 70 多座帝王陵寝，以及众多国宝级古建筑。

Rich in cultural tourist resources, Shaanxi is home to over 70 mausoleums, including those of the Yellow Emperor, the Yandi Emperor, the Emperor Qinshihuang, and emperors of the Han and the Tang dynasties, as well as many ancient architectural complexes that can be regarded as national treasures.

西安城墙

中国现存规模最大、保存最完整的古代城垣——西安明城墙与护城河及环城公园组成了西安市最具特色的一大景观。

位于市中心的钟楼与鼓楼是西安的标志性建筑，这两座明代建筑遥相呼应，蔚

Xi'an City Wall is the biggest and best-preserved ancient city wall still extant in China. The City Wall, together with the moat and annular park, forms a part of the fantastic scenery of Xi'an.

Situated at the center of Xi'an, the Bell Tower and the Drum Tower are landmark buildings of the city. The two majestic Ming Dynasty buildings echo each

长安十二时辰主题街区主题演出

在长安十二时辰主题街区，人们身着汉服拍照

为壮观。

大雁塔与小雁塔是佛塔这种古印度佛寺的建筑形式融入华夏文化的典型物证。

华清宫也称华清池，位于西安市临潼区，其以唐明皇与杨贵妃缠绵的爱情故事和震惊中外的西安事变而蜚声天下。

大唐芙蓉园仿照唐代皇家园林建造，是中国第一个全方位展示盛唐风貌的大型皇家园林式文化主题公园。

从魏晋南北朝到隋唐时期，长安一直是汉传佛教的活动中心，留下了法门寺、草堂寺等大量祖庭寺庙。

other from afar.

Both the Giant Wild Goose Pagoda and the Small Wild Goose Pagoda are representative physical evidence of the fusion of the ancient Indian Buddhist temples' architectural form with Chinese culture.

Situated at Lintong District, Xi'an, the Huaqing Palace is also known as the Huaqing Pool. The palace is famed for the sentimental love story between Emperor Minghuang of the Tang Dynasty and his concubine Yang as well as the world-shaking Xi'an Incident.

The Tang Paradise was rebuilt according to the style of imperial gardens on its site of the Tang Dynasty. It is China's first large scale imperial garden-themed park that showcases the prosperity of the Tang Dynasty comprehensively.

Chang'an had been an important center of Buddhism from the Wei, Jin, Southern and Northern dynasties to the Sui and the Tang dynasties, and left many ancestral temples such as Famen Temple and Caotang Temple.

山水之旅
Landscape Tourism

陕西地形狭长，地貌多样，特殊的地理环境造就了陕西集高原沟壑、平原沃野和江南水乡风光于一体的多彩景象。

陕北山峦起伏，沟壑纵横，气象壮美；八百里秦川横亘关中，平川与黄土塬地交错铺排，相映成趣；陕南青山绿水，风景如画，湖光山色相映生辉，峡谷溶洞遍布

Shaanxi Province, which is long and narrow in its topography, boasts a wealth of unique landforms, and integrates the northwestern scenery with the southern scenery to create a colorful and fantastic view.

Northern Shaanxi, boasting continuous mountains and valleys, is a majestic view. A 400 km-long section of the Qinling Mountain Range runs across the Guanzhong region where the plains and plateaus interlace with each other. Southern

秦岭秋韵

其间。

　　黄河、渭水、汉江风貌各异，既有雄浑壮阔的磅礴之美，也有蜿蜒曲折的秀丽旖旎。

　　秦岭横亘于中国中部，面积广大，气势磅礴，被誉为"国家中央公园"。2009年，陕西秦岭终南山

Shaanxi features green hills mirrored in the crystal rivers and picturesque scenery dotted with lakes, mountains, canyons and water-eroded caves.

The Yellow River, the Weihe River and the Hanjiang River are characterized with their distinctive majestic beauty and winding charm.

The Qinling Mountain Range is located in central China as a range of vast, grand and majestic mountains, enjoying the fame of "National Central Park". In 2009,

地质公园入选世界地质公园。太白山为秦岭最高峰,自古以来就以高、寒、险、奇、富饶、神秘闻名于世。"太白积雪六月天"是著名的"长安八景"之一。

Shaanxi Qinling Zhongnanshan Geopark was listed as one of the world geoparks. Mount Taibai, the highest peak of the Qinling Mountain Range, has been famed for its height, coldness, steepness, fertility and mystery from ancient times. The "Snow-capped Mount Taibai in Summer" is one of the top eight scenic attractions of Chang'an.

As one of the five famous mountains in China, Mount

汉中红寺湖

华山是中国五大名山之一，海拔2154米。华山挺拔险峻，终年云蒸霞蔚，南接秦岭，北瞰黄渭，扼大西北进出中原的门户，素有"奇险天下第一山"之称。

Hua has an altitude of 2,154 meters. Being an upright, steep mountain perennially capped with clouds, it connects the Qinling Mountain Range in the south, overlooks the Yellow River and the Weihe River in the north, and guards the plain in the Great Northwest. It has long been given the name of "The Number One Most Dangerous Mountain under Heaven".

2024 中国陕西
2024 China Shaanxi

博物馆之旅
Museum Tourism

陕西被誉为中国天然历史博物馆，文化遗存丰富，文物点密度大、数量多、等级高，拥有中国各个历史时期具有代表性的文物古迹。陕西目前有9家国家一级博物馆和数十家免费博物馆，全面展示了三秦大地悠久的历史和灿烂辉煌的文化。

Shaanxi is known as China's "natural history museum". The cultural relics and historical ruins found here are concentrated, numerous and representative, encompassing almost every historical period in Chinese history. It is home to nine state first-level museums and dozens of free museums which comprehensively reflect China's long history and splendid culture.

Shaanxi History Museum is China's first large scale national museum equipped with modern facilities. It

秦始皇陵兵马俑

陕西历史博物馆是中国第一座大型现代化国家级博物馆，馆藏文物时间跨度长达100多万年。其中汉唐金银器独步全国，唐墓壁画举世无双，被誉为"古都明珠，华夏宝库"。

陕西历史博物馆秦汉馆（简称

collects cultural relics with a time span of over one million years. The gold and silver wares of the Han and the Tang dynasties are the most exquisite in China. The murals from the Tang tombs are unrivaled in the world. The museum is honored "Pearl of Xi'an and treasure of China".

The Qin Han Museum of the Shaanxi History Museum, located in the Qinhan New City of Xi-xian New Area, is currently the only museum in China showcasing the origin, development, and contributions of civilization of the Qin and

游客在陕西历史博物馆秦汉馆参观

"陕历博秦汉馆")位于西咸新区秦汉新城,是目前国内唯一一座以集中展示秦汉文明的缘起、发展、贡献为宗旨的博物馆。

陕西考古博物馆是一座大型考古类专题博物馆,收纳陕西省各地各个时期的出土文物10万余件,展陈真实还原出土现场、揭示演进变化、展现保护修复、系统体现历史进程,展现了陕西这片古老的土地中埋藏着的华夏文明最精彩的记忆。

the Han dynasties.

The Shaanxi Archaeology Museum is a large-scale archeology-themed museum with a collection of more than 100,000 pieces of unearthed cultural relics from various historical periods in Shaanxi Province. By restoring the site of the unearthed cultural relics, showing the protection and restoration of cultural relics, and revealing the evolution and changes of history, this museum boasts the most wonderful memories of Chinese civilization buried in this ancient land of Shaanxi Province.

The Xi'an Branch of National Archives of Publications and Culture,(also known as Wenji Pavilion), one of the three branches of the China National Archives of Publications and Culture, is located in Guifeng Mountain,

游客在咸阳博物院参观龙文化展览

中国国家版本馆西安分馆（文济阁）为中国国家版本馆"一总三分"分馆之一，坐落在陕西境内秦岭北侧的圭峰山。高台筑阁，次第错落，形成中轴对称、主从有序的建筑序列，呈现出磅礴的汉唐风格。

秦始皇兵马俑博物馆是建立在兵马俑原址上的遗址性博物馆。博物馆的一、二、三号坑中发掘出了 7000 多尊列为军阵的兵马俑。兵马俑是世界考古史上最伟大的发现之一，1987 年，联合国教科文组织将秦始皇陵及兵马俑坑列入世界文化遗产名录。

north of the Qinling Mountains in Shaanxi Province. Hathpaces and pavilions are built in a staggered manner, forming a symmetrical and orderly sequence with a central axis, fully showing majesty of the Han and Tang dynasties.

Emperor Qinshihuang's Terracotta Warriors and Horses Museum is built on the original pit for the terracotta warriors and horses. More than 7,000 vivid terracotta warriors and horses with various postures in arrays were unearthed from the Pits No.1, 2 and 3. It is one of the greatest discoveries in the world archaeological history. In 1987, UNESCO inscribed the Terracotta Warriors and Horses and the Mausoleum of Emperor

宝鸡青铜器博物院

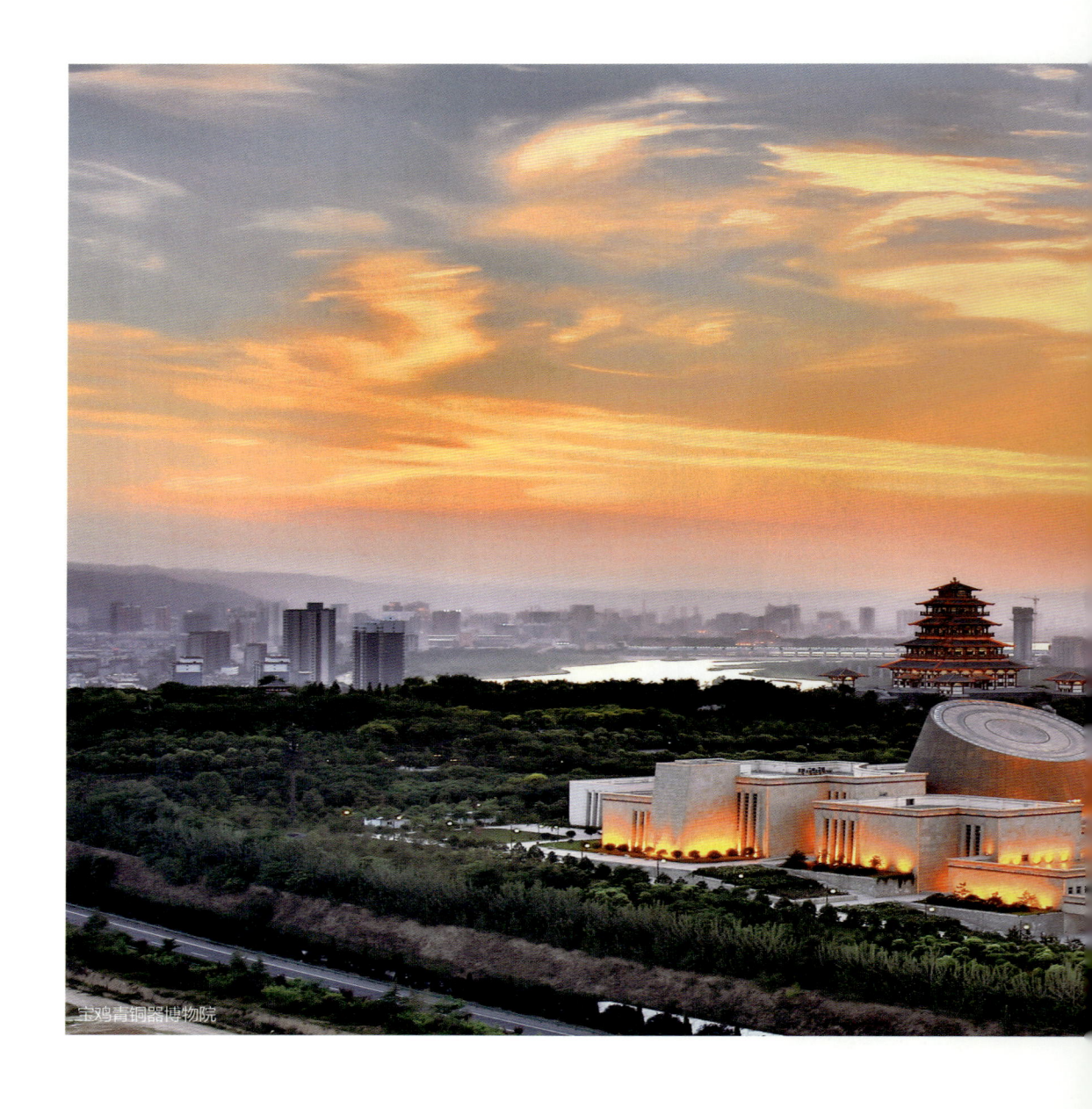

西安碑林博物馆是陕西创建最早的博物馆，以收藏、陈列和研究历代碑刻、墓志及石刻为主，因碑石如林，故名碑林。著名的《开成石经》《大秦景教流行中国碑》《昭陵六骏》中的四骏等文物均藏于此馆。

Qinshihuang into the World Cultural Heritage List.

Xi'an Beilin Museum （Forest of Stone Steles Museum） is the earliest museum in Shaanxi. It mainly focuses on the collection, exhibition and research of steles, epitaphs and stone inscriptions. It gets the name Beilin from the Chinese meaning of forest of stone steles. The famous "Kaicheng Stone Sutra", "Stele for the Spread of Cippus Nestorianism in China" and four steeds of the Six

延安革命纪念馆位于延安市宝塔区，是中华人民共和国成立后最早建立的革命纪念馆之一。纪念馆展出大量珍贵的革命文物、文献和照片，生动、形象地再现了老一辈革命家的光辉业绩。

Steeds of Zhao Mausoleum are collected in the museum.

Yan'an Revolutionary Memorial, located in Baota District, Yan'an City, is one of the earliest revolutionary memorials built after the founding of the People's Republic of China. It exhibits numerous valuable revolutionary relics, literature and photos, vividly representing the glorious feats of the older generation of revolutionary leaders.

千年古都，常来长安
——大唐不夜城

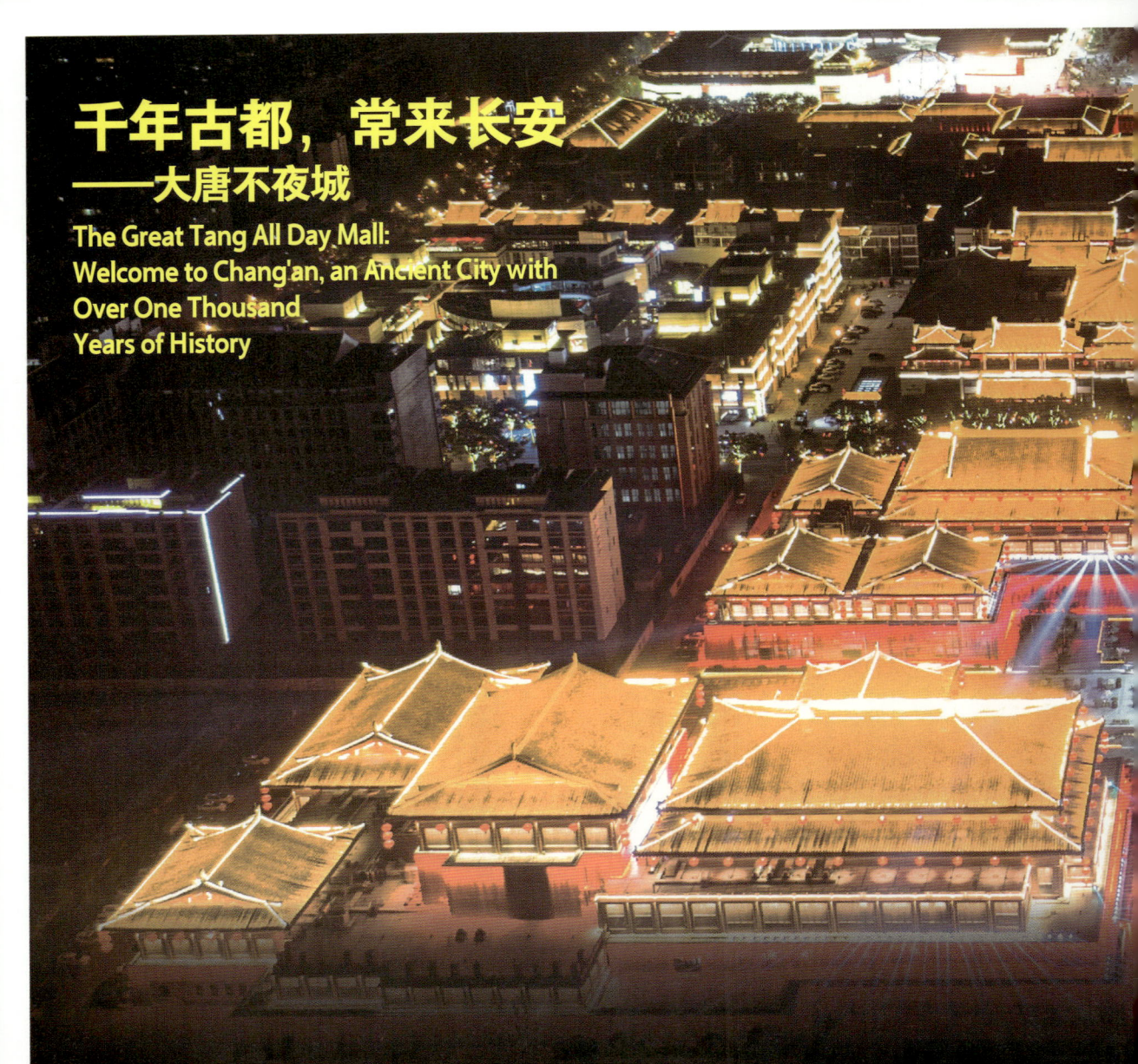

The Great Tang All Day Mall: Welcome to Chang'an, an Ancient City with Over One Thousand Years of History

　　提起西安，不由得就会想到在中国历史上占有重要地位的大唐，而位于西安大雁塔脚下的大唐不夜城，就是一个融合了大唐盛世风情的文化旅游胜地。

　　大唐不夜城位于陕西省西安市雁塔区的大雁塔脚下，北起大雁塔南广场，南至唐城墙遗址，东起慈恩东路，西至慈恩西路，街区南北长2100米，东西宽500米，总建筑面积65万平方米。

　　大唐不夜城以唐风元素为主线，建有大雁塔北广场、玄奘广场、贞观广场、创领新时代广场四大广场，西安音乐厅、陕西大剧院、西安美术馆、曲江太平洋电影城等四座文化场馆，大唐佛文化、大唐群英谱、贞观之治、武后行从、开元盛世等五大文化雕塑。

　　One cannot mention Xi'an without thinking of the Great Tang Dynasty, which holds an important position in Chinese history. And the Great Tang All Day Mall, located at the foot of the Giant Wild Goose Pagoda in Xi'an, is a cultural tourist site integrating the charm of the Great Tang Dynasty.

　　Located at the foot of the Great Wild Goose Pagoda in Yanta District, Xi'an, Shaanxi Province, the Great Tang All Day Mall starts from the South Plaza of the Giant Wild Goose Pagoda in the north to the Ruins of the Tang City Wall in the south, from Ci'en Rd(E) in the east to Ci'en Rd(W) in the west. It is a block of 2,100 meters from north to south and 500 meters from east to west, covering 650,000 square kilometers in total.

　　With the Tang style as the theme, the Great Tang All Day Mall has four major plazas: the North Plaza of the Great Wild Goose Pagoda, Xuanzang Plaza, Zhenguan Plaza and Chuangling Times Plaza; four major cultural venues: Xi'an Concert Hall, Shaanxi Opera House, Xi'an Art Museum, and Qu Jiang Movie

大唐不夜城中轴景观大道是一条2100米长、纵贯南北的中央雕塑景观步行街，是亚洲最大的景观大道，展示了以李世民、李隆基、武则天、玄奘等一代帝王、历史人物为主题的大唐群英谱雕塑。在这里，九组雕塑群与现代化的水景系统、灯光系统、立体交通系统相结合，立体呈现大唐帝国在宗教、文学、艺术、科技等领域的地位，彰显大国气象，多维再现盛世大唐风范。

大唐不夜城展现了千年古都的历史命脉和文化轴线，凸显了西安的城市精神风貌与文化气韵，已然成为城市的一张新名片。

City Pacific Cineplex; and five great cultural sculptures: Buddhist Culture in the Tang Dynasty, Heroes of the Tang Dynasty, Prosperity of Zhenguan, Empress Wu Zetian's Tour of Inspection, and the Flourishing Kaiyuan Reign.

The Central Landscape Avenue of the Great Tang All Day Mall is a 2100-meter-long pedestrian street from north to south with sculptures along the middle line. As the largest landscape avenue in Asia, it displays sculptures of heroes in the Tang Dynasty with emperors and historical figures including Li Shimin, Li Longji, Wu Zetian, Xuanzang and their heroic stories. Here, nine groups of sculptures are integrated with modern waterscape, lighting and three-dimensional traffic systems to present the achievements of the Great Tang Empire in religion, literature, art, science and technology, showing the image of a powerful nation and reproducing the spectacle of the Great Tang Dynasty in multiple dimensions.

The Great Tang All Day Mall shows the history and culture of this ancient capital with over one thousand years of history, highlighting the urban spirit and cultural charm of Xi'an, and has become a new label of this city.

从"绿水青山就是金山银山"到"人不负青山，青山定不负人"，陕西坚持绿色发展的思路愈发清晰，生态保护的成效愈加显著。

From the concept that "lush mountains and lucid waters are invaluable assets" to the philosophy that "if we do not fail Nature, nature shall never fail us", Shaanxi has become more confident in its commitment to green development and has made significant achievements in ecological protection.

>

Chapter Two

第二篇

青山绿水，持续发展

林间新绿一重重

Lush Mountains and Lucid Waters for Sustainable Development

New Green Leaves Throbbing among Branches

国土增绿
Land Greening

陕西省制定《陕西省国土绿化规划（2023—2030年）》，实现造林种草落地上图入库。2023年，全省营造林522万多亩，种草改良33万多亩，治理沙化土地94.9万亩，超额完成年度任务，造

The Land Greening Planning of Shaanxi Province (2023–2030) was formulated to ensure that afforestation and grass planting were fully implemented and input into the digital map and the data base. In 2023, more than 5.22 million *mu* of afforestation has been planted in Shaanxi Province, together with over 330,000 *mu* of grassland planted and improved, and 949,000 *mu* of desertified land put under control, over fulfilling the task of the year and ranking among the top across the country in the afforestation area. The actual afforestation and greening fiscal funds exceeded 1.1 billion *yuan*, and efforts were made to invest more than 1.6 billion *yuan* in two major national projects for the protection and restoration of important ecosystems, ranking among the top in the country for three consecutive years. Yulin

林面积居全国前列。落实造林绿化财政资金超过11亿元，争取"双重"项目资金投入超过16亿元，连续三年位居全国前列。榆林市成功纳入国土绿化试点示范项目，新增全国森林可持续经营试点9个。建立林业、自然资源部门造林落地上图图斑联合会审制度，坚决杜绝违规占用耕地绿化造林。

陕西省委、省政府召开全省荒漠化综合防治和黄河"几字弯"攻坚战工作会议，总结多年来特别是党的十八大以来防沙治沙成绩，安

has been successfully incorporated into the national land greening pilot demonstration construction, and has added nine new national forest sustainable management pilots. In addition, a joint review system has been established for the implementation and input of afforestation into the digital map with the forestry and natural resources departments to resolutely prevent illegal occupation of cultivated land for afforestation.

The Shaanxi Provincial Party Committee and the Provincial Government held a conference on the comprehensive prevention and control of desertification along the "S-shape" section of the Yellow River, summarizing the achievements of desertification control

退耕还林后的陕北

排部署当前和今后一个时期的工作。制定《陕西省荒漠化综合防治和黄河"几字弯"攻坚战行动方案（2021—2030年）》，明确"创造防沙治沙新奇迹、力争在西部做示范"的战略定位、两步走目标任务、"三区三战"总体布局

over the years, especially since the 18th National Congress of the CPC, and arranging and deploying the current and future work. Efforts have been made to formulate the *Action Plan for Comprehensive Prevention and Control of Desertification in Shaanxi Province and the Battle along the "S-shape" Section of the Yellow River (2021-2030)*, clarifying the two-step goals and tasks, overall layout of three areas (Mu Us Sandland Sand Prevention and Control Area, Loess Plateau Soil and Water Loss Comprehensive Management Area, and Guanzhong Ecological and Economic Collaborative Promotion Area) and three battles for

和12项重点行动。组织召开全省科学绿化暨黄河"几字弯"攻坚战推进会,全面铺开全省荒漠化综合防治和黄河"几字弯"攻坚战建设工作。《陕西省防沙治沙规划》获国家批复并印发实施。

comprehensive control of moving sandland, desertified land, and vegetation restoration in the Weibei arid plateau), 12 key actions and the strategic positioning of "creating a new miracle of desertification prevention and control and striving to be a demonstration in Western China". A meeting was organized for the scientific land greening and the battle along the "S-shape" section of the Yellow River to comprehensively implement the prevention and control of desertification in Shaanxi Province and the construction of the "S-shape" section of the Yellow River. At the same time, the *Desertification Prevention and Control Plan of Shaanxi Province* has been approved by the state and issued for implementation.

绿意盎然的乾坤湾

生物保护
Biological Conservation

陕西省印发《关于陆生野生动物禁猎区禁猎期的通告》《关于严禁破坏野生动植物资源的通告》，持续开展"清风""排查整治乱捕滥猎候鸟"等专项行动。加强重大陆生野生动物疫源疫病监测防控，2023年全年未发生野生动物传染性疾病。调查监测显示，陕西分布

Shaanxi Province issued the "Notice on the Closed Hunting Period of Land Wildlife Sanctuaries" and "Notice on the Prohibition of Destroying Wildlife Resources", and continued to carry out special actions such as "clearing action" and "investigation and rectification of illegal hunting of migratory birds". Efforts were made to strengthen the monitoring and prevention of major terrestrial wildlife infectious diseases, and no wild animal infectious diseases have occurred throughout

秦岭大熊猫

朱鹮

的大熊猫、朱鹮、秦岭冷杉等12种极度濒危野生动植物种群数量大幅增长。

2023年，秦岭大熊猫研究中心人工繁育大熊猫4胎7仔，创历史最好成绩，秦岭大熊猫人工圈养种群达49只。首次在延安南泥湾、榆林横山区开展高寒地区朱鹮再引入试验。在秦岭北麓蓝田段野化放飞朱鹮23只，

the whole year. According to the survey, the population of 12 endangered wild animals and plants distributed in Shaanxi, including giant pandas, crested ibis, and Qinling fir, has significantly increased.

In 2023, the Qinling Giant Panda Research Center has 4 litters of 7 pandas bred in captivity, the best result in history. In total, there are 49 pandas in captivity in the Qinling Mountain Range. In addition, the reintroduction experiment of crested ibis in the alpine region was carried out for the first time in Nanniwan,

金丝猴

全省朱鹮野外种群数量达6600余只，全球朱鹮种群数量突破1万只。国家林业和草原局朱鹮保护国家创新联盟挂牌成立，国家级秦岭大熊猫繁育基地、国家林业和草原局朱鹮保护研究中心筹建工作稳步推进。

Yan'an and Hengshan District, Yulin. 23 ibises were released in the wild at the northern foot of the Qinling Mountain Range, with the number of ibises rising to more than 6,600 and the global population exceeding 10,000. The National Innovation Alliance for Crested Ibis Conservation of the National Forestry and Grassland Administration was established, and the preparatory work for the establishment of the National Qinling Base of Giant Panda Breeding and the Crested Ibis Conservation and Research Center of National Forestry and Grassland Administration has been steadily progressing.

羚牛

河流与湿地
Rivers and Wetlands

近年来，陕西省牢固树立"绿水青山就是金山银山"理念，把生态文明建设放在全局重要位置审视和推进，把湿地保护作为黄河流域生态保护、当好秦岭卫士、确保一泓清水永续北上的重要抓手，扎实

In recent years, Shaanxi Province has been fully adhering to the concept that lucid waters and lush mountains are invaluable assets, and has placed the ecological conservation in an important position in the overall situation. Shaanxi has also gained significant achievements in regarding wetland protection as a major part of the ecological protection of the Yellow River Basin and the Qinling Mountain Range, ensuring the clarity of the river for the water diversion project

综合整治后的汉江汉中城市段

推动湿地保护工作走深走实，取得了明显成效。

2022年以来，修订颁布《陕西省湿地保护条例》《陕西省省级重要湿地管理办法》等法规制度，湿地分级管理体系逐步完善，加快推动湿地

to the north, and promoting the wetland protection.

Since 2022, laws and regulations such as the Wetland Protection Regulations of Shaanxi Province and the Measures for the Management of Provincial Important Wetlands of Shaanxi Province have been revised and promulgated. The wetland classification management system has been gradually improved, thus accelerating the ecological restoration of wetlands, leading to restoration

生态修复建设，修复退化湿地1.6万亩，7处国家湿地公园试点通过验收。

2023年以来，新增国家重要湿地1处，实施小流域综合治理149条，新增水土流失治理面积4008平方千米。黄河流域65

of 16,000 *mu* of degraded wetlands and 7 pilot national wetland parks passing the acceptance check.

Since 2023, one national key wetland has been added with 149 small river basins comprehensively managed, and an additional 4,008 square kilometers of soil erosion brought under control. The water quality at the state-monitored sections of the mainstream of the Yellow River witnessed 95.4% in Grade Ⅰ-Ⅲ, no cross-section water body quality lower than Class Ⅴ. The water quality

汉中南湖风光

个国控断面中，Ⅰ—Ⅲ类比例达95.4%，无劣Ⅴ类断面，黄河（陕西段）、渭河、延河等主要干、支流水质全部为优。长江流域46个国控断面Ⅰ—Ⅲ类比例达100%，汉江、丹江、嘉陵江水质持续为优，出省断面水质持续保持Ⅱ类以上。

of the main branches and tributaries of the Yellow River (Shaanxi section), the Weihe River and the Yanhe River are all excellent. The proportion of Grade I-III level in 46 state-controlled sections in the Yangtze River Basin has reached 100%. In addition, the water quality of the Hanjiang River, Danjiang River and Jialingjiang River continues to be excellent, with the water quality of the cross-section out of the province remaining above Grade II level.

诗经故里——合阳湿地
The Cradle of *The Book of Songs*: Heyang Wetland

合阳是黄河岸边的"诗经之城"。"关关雎鸠，在河之洲"，《诗经》开篇所描写的地方就位于合阳的洽川黄河湿地。

作为黄河流域面积最大的温泉湖泊型湿地，"万顷芦荡、千眼神泉、百种珍禽、十里荷塘、一条黄河、秦晋相望"是洽川黄河湿地的真实写照。洽川黄河湿地包括瀵泉、黄河魂、福山、莘国水城等，其中最吸引人的自然是堪称洽川传奇的瀵泉。

瀵泉是洽川独有的景观。所谓瀵泉，即指泉水从地下喷出，"大如车轮，状似沸腾"。这样的瀵泉景观洽川有很多，最著名的有七眼：东鲤瀵、西鲤瀵、王村瀵、子瀵、夏阳瀵、渤池瀵、熨斗瀵。

Located on the bank of the Yellow River, Heyang is reputed as "the city of *the Book of Songs*". "are cooing/A pair, A pair of turtle-doves." The place described in the first song of *the Book of Songs* is Hechuan Yellow River Wetland.

As the largest lake wetland with hot spring in the Yellow River Basin, Hechuan Yellow River Wetland enjoys "10,000 hectares of reeds, 1,000 springs, 100 kinds of rare birds, 10-*li* lotus ponds and the Yellow River connecting Qin (Shaanxi Province) and Jin (Shanxi Province)." Hechuan Yellow River Wetland includes the Fen Spring, the Yellow River Soul (a water conservancy scenic area), Mount Fu, Shenguo Water City, etc, among which the most attractive one is the Fen Spring, renowned as the legendary of Hechuan.

The Fen Spring is a unique scenery of Hechuan. The term "Fen Spring" means the spring water spurting out from underground, looking like "boiling water as big as wheels." There are many such

当地人更愿意将东鲤瀵称为处女泉，因为这里流传着周文王与太姒相识相恋的传说。"窈窕淑女，君子好逑。"周文王与太姒纯真唯美的爱情故事在这片土地上已经吟唱了几千年。

当地还因此形成了千年风俗，出嫁前的姑娘要来此沐浴，以祈求灵泉滋润。处女泉源远流长的历史气韵与四季各异的醉人景观吸引了众多游人的目光。

这里拥有世界上最神奇的瀵水温泉，更有万里黄河极致的浪漫体验。

自然景观与人文景观交融，历史遗迹和现代工程互为映衬、浑然一体，使人切实感受到大自然之鬼斧神工，尽享江南水乡情趣。

springs in Hechuan, seven of which are most famous: the Dongli Fen, the Xili Fen, the Wangcun Fen, Zi Fen, the Xiayang Fen, the Bochi Fen, and the Yundou Fen.

The local people prefer to call the Dongli Fen Spring as the Virgin Spring because of a prevailing legend that King Wen of the Zhou Dynasty and Taisi met and fell in love here. "A good young man is wooing/A fair maiden he loves." The pure and beautiful love story of King Wen of the Zhou Dynasty and Taisi has been sung in this land for thousands of years.

The local people have even formed a custom for this legend over the past thousands of years. Before getting married, girls will come here and take a bath for the nourishment of the spring. The Virgin Spring has attracted a lot of visitors for its profound history and charming scenery in different seasons.

Here people can enjoy the most magical hot spring in the world with water gushing from the underground, and get some extremely romantic experience along the mighty Yellow River.

With the combination of natural scenery and cultural sights, the historical relics and modern buildings are integrated together, making people feel nature's magic and enjoy the fun of canal towns.

洽川湿地

面对科技革命和产业变革的加速演进,陕西大力发展县域经济、民营经济、开放型经济、数字经济,经济结构持续优化,内生动力显著增强,高质量发展扎实推进。

In the face of rapid development of technological revolution and industrial transformation, Shaanxi has made great efforts to develop the county economy, private economy, open economy and digital economy, leading to the continuously optimized economic structure, significantly enhanced endogenous driving force and solidly promoted high-quality development.

>

Chapter Three

第三篇

蓬勃生机，开拓进取

晴空一鹤排云上

Booming with Vitality and Forging Ahead

A Crane Flapping Its Wings to the Clear Sky

发展潜力
Development Potential

紧盯关键环节 稳定经济运行
Focusing on Key Links to Stabilize Economic Processes

2023年，陕西坚持能源与非能稳产并举抓工业，巴拉素等10处煤矿建成、释放产能3145万吨，延长气田扩产一期项目新增产能18.9亿方，新增电力装机1520万千瓦、其中光伏809万千瓦，新能源装机总量突破4000万千瓦，外送电量797亿千瓦时、增长

32%，镇安抽水蓄能电站 1 号机组调试发电，陕皖电力通道获批，榆能 40 万吨乙二醇项目建成，4 个千亿级现代能化项目前期工作取得实质性进展，汽车、太阳能电池、集成电路圆片产量分别增长 33.4%、154.5%、7.4%，新增规上工业企业 1000 家左右，规上工业增加值增长

In 2023, Shaanxi Province insisted on the stability of energy and non-energy industries to promote industrial development. Specifically, 10 coal mines including Balasu have been built and released with a production capacity of 31.45 million tons. The first phase of the gas field expansion project in Yanchang has added a production capacity of 1.89 billion cubic meters, with an additional installed power of 15.2 million kilowatts, including 8.09 million kilowatts of photovoltaic power. The total installed capacity of new energy has exceeded 40 million kilowatts, and the exported electricity has reached 79.7 billion kilowatt hours, an increase of 32%. At the same time, the No. 1 Zhen'an pumped storage power station has undergone commissioning and power

西安高新区

5%，其中装备制造业增长12.5%。强化"四个一批"项目全周期动态管理，投资130亿元的比亚迪扩产项目当年开工、当年投产，G8.5+基板玻璃项目建成，延榆高铁开工建设，西延、西十、西渝高铁和西安东站、西安咸阳国际机场三期等重大项目按时间节点推进，丹

generation. The Shaanxi Anhui power channel has been approved, along with the completion of the 400,000 tons ethylene glycol project of Yulin Energy Group. Substantial progress has been made in the preliminary work of four modern energy projects worth billions of yuan. The production of automobiles, solar cells, and integrated circuit wafers increased by 33.4%, 154.5%, and 7.4% respectively. About 1000 new industrial companies above designated scale were added, with a 5% increase in added value, including a 12.5% increase in equipment manufacturing. Efforts have been made to strengthen the dynamic management of the projects throughout the entire cycle in the preparation, commencement, development and completion of a series of major projects. The BYD expansion project with an investment of 13 billion *yuan* was launched and put into operation in the same year. The G8.5+substrate glass project

工业机器人在陕汽生产线上作业

凤至山阳高速公路通车，引汉济渭工程实现供水。举办"秦乐购"消费促进活动，新能源汽车销售额同比增长100.3%，限上住宿业、餐饮业营业额分别增长24.4%、19.6%。游客人数、旅游收入分别增长106.5%、150.6%，文旅重点产业链年综合收入达到7729亿元。

was completed. The construction of the Yan'an-Yulin high-speed railway commenced, and major projects such as the Xi'an-Yan'an, Xi'an-Shiyan, Xi'an-Chongqing high-speed railway, Xi'an East Station, and Xi'an Xianyang International Airport Phase III were promoted according to time nodes. The Danfeng-Shanyang Expressway was open to traffic, and the Hanjiang to Weihe River Project achieved water supply. In addition, the "Qin Happy Shopping" consumer promotion campaign was held. The sales of new energy vehicles increased by 100.3%, while the revenue of the accommodation and catering industries increased by 24.4% and 19.6% respectively. The number of tourists and tourism revenue increased by 106.5% and 150.6% respectively, and the annual comprehensive income of the key cultural and tourism industry chain reached 772.9 billion *yuan*.

坚持创新驱动　推动产业升级
Upholding the Innovation Drive to Promote Industrial Upgrading

2023年，陕西出台西安"双中心"建设支持政策，高精度地基授时系统主体完工，阿秒激光项目获批。一体推进省级"两链"融合专项和"揭榜挂帅"项目，攻克关键核心技术363项，延长煤油气综合利用项目获中国工业大奖，宝石机械特深井自动化钻机等一批国际首台（套）装备成功研制并应用，国内首条千吨级高品质镁示范线建成投产。以"三项改革"放大秦创原效能，创新平台帮助企业解决难题900余个，新增国家级科技孵化器10个，科研人员成立转化企业1051家，科技型中小企业、高新

In 2023, Shaanxi introduced the "dual center" construction in Xi'an, with the main body of the high-precision ground-based timing system completed and the attosecond laser project officially sanctioned. Efforts have been made to promote the provincial "industry and innovation" integration and "science and technology reward" project, thus overcoming 363 key core technologies. Specifically, the Yanchang coal, petroleum and gas comprehensive utilization project won the China Industry Award, along with the gem mechanical ultra-deep well automatic drilling rig and a number of international first equipment (sets) successfully launched and put into application. In addition, the first thousand-ton high-quality magnesium demonstration line in China was completed and put into operation. With the reforms in three aspects of labor, personnel and distribution, the efficiency of Qin Chuangyuan has been put into full play in helping more than 900 enterprises solve

西安电子谷核心区已初具规模

技术企业分别增长37%、33%，新增国家专精特新"小巨人"企业40家。全省发明专利授权2.2万件、增长16.1%，有效发明专利拥有量突破10万件，专利质押融资1204项、54.7亿元，技术合同成交额达到4120亿元、增长34.9%，就地转化技术合同占比提高11个百分点。加快发展先进制造业和战略性新兴产业，制造业、科学研究和技术服务业企业投资分别增长10.1%、46.2%，制造业重点产业链产值突破1万亿元、增长10.2%，乘用车（新能源）、太阳能光伏等9条产业链产值增速超过两位数。大力发展数字经济，国家超算西安中心、未来人工智能计算中心等新型算力基础设施建成投用，5家企业入选全国智能制造示范工厂揭榜单位，数字产品制造重点行业增加值增长18%。

秦创原·氢合湾氢能双链融合科创区

problems. In addition, 10 new state-level science and technology incubators were established, along with 1,051 transformation enterprises established by researchers. The high-tech small and medium-sized enterprises and new high-tech enterprises increased by 37% and 33% respectively, and 40 new national specialized "little giant" firms were added. 22,000 invention patents were authorized throughout the whole province, an increase of 16.1%. The number of effective invention patents exceeded 100,000, and 1204 patents were pledged for financing, totaling 5.47 billion *yuan*. At the same time, the transaction volume of technology contracts reached 412 billion *yuan*, an increase of 34.9%, and the proportion of on-site conversion technology contracts increased by 11 percentage points. The government has accelerated the development of advanced manufacturing and strategic emerging industries, with investment on manufacturing, scientific research, and technology service enterprises increasing by 10.1% and 46.2% respectively. The output value of key manufacturing industry chains has exceeded 1 trillion *yuan*, an increase of 10.2%. The growth rate of nine industrial chains; including passenger vehicles (new energy) and solar photovoltaics, has exceeded 10 percent. In addition to this, the digital economy has been vigorously developed, with new arithmetic infrastructures such as the National Supercomputer Center in Xi'an and the Future Artificial Intelligence Computing Centre being built and put into operation. Meanwhile, five enterprises were selected as national intelligent manufacturing demonstration factory units, and the added-value of key industries in digital product manufacturing increased by 18%.

推进改革开放 释放市场活力
Promoting Reform and Opening up to Unleash Market Vitality

2023年，陕西大力发展民营经济，推广运用"陕企通""秦务员""秦政通"一体化服务平台，上线"一件事一次办"服务事项15个，"跨省通办"政务事项达到154项。实施"三整治四提升"专项行动，经营主体满意度达到94.4%。新增减税降费及退税缓费超490亿元，普惠小微贷款、制造业中长期贷款分别增长26.2%、26.9%，实有企业156.5万户、增长12.1%，净增"五上"民营企业1182家，新增上市企业7家。持续推动"亩均论英雄"综合改革，供应工业"标准地"316宗3.6万亩，"交地即交证"项目676个，要素保障和土地集约利用水平进一步提高。启动新一轮国企改革深化提升行动，组建水务发展集团，省属企业实现利润799.4亿元，居全国第六位。积极落实中国一中

In 2023, Shaanxi Province vigorously developed the private economy, promoted the use of integrated service platforms such as "Shaan Qitong", "Qin Wuyuan" and "Qin Zhengtong", and put on line "All-in-One-Go" service for 15 items, and "inter-provincial government services" are provided for 154 items. The government has carried out a special campaign of "rectification of three aspects and upgrading of four aspects", stepped up efforts to clear up arrears of corporate accounts, and notified 10 typical cases of damaging the business environment. Through these efforts, the satisfaction of business entities reached 94.4%. At the same time, the new tax and fee cuts, tax reimbursement and deferred fees exceeded 49 billion *yuan*, and inclusive small and micro loans, manufacturing medium and long-term loans increased by 26.2% and 26.9% respectively, totaling 1.565 million enterprises, an increase of 12.1%. and a net increase of 1182 private enterprises and seven new listed companies. Sustained efforts were made to promote the comprehensive reform of "valuing work effectiveness per land unit", providing 316 standard industrial land plots of 36,000 *mu*, issuing certificates to 676 projects along with land transfer, and further improving factor protection and

"秦务员"给三秦百姓带来惊喜

运维人员在中国移动（陕西西咸新区）数据中心进行运维巡检

亚峰会涉陕成果，实现中亚五国通航全覆盖，对中亚出口增长221.9%。大力发展开放型经济，中欧班列开行量突破5300列、增长15.3%，出口陕西货值增长26.1%，自贸试验区4项改革创新经验在全国推广，新增有业绩的外贸企业368家，陕汽重卡、新能源汽车出口分别增长101.4%、1154%。高水平举办丝博会、欧亚经济论坛、杨凌农高会等，赴长三角、粤港澳大湾区开展招商推介，西安闪存芯片、咸阳高端铜箔材料、杨凌麦肯食品、太古里文化商业等一批重大外资项目相继落地，新设外商投资企业增长29.9%，实际使用内资增长12.6%。

land intensive utilization. A new round of deepening state-owned enterprise reform has been launched, together with the forming of the Water Development Group. Provincial enterprises have achieved a profit of 79.94 billion *yuan*, ranking sixth in the whole country. Efforts have been made to actively implement the achievements of the China-Central Asia Summit related to Shaanxi, achieving full coverage of navigation in the five Central Asian countries, and increasing exports to Central Asia by 221.9%. Great efforts have been made to develop an open economy, with over 5,300 trips of China-Europe Railway Express, an increase of 15.3%. Four reform and innovation experience cases in Shaanxi Pilot Free Trade Zone have been promoted throughout the country. At the same time, there were 368 new foreign trade enterprises with performance. Shaanxi Automobile Heavy Truck and new energy vehicle exports increased by 101.4% and 1154% respectively. At the same time, a series of high-level conferences were held, including the Silk Road International Expo, Eurasian Economic Forum, Yangling Agriculture Conference, etc., in addition to investment promotion meetings in the Yangtze River Delta and the Guangdong-Hong Kong-Macao Greater Bay Area. A number of major foreign investment projects such as Xi'an Flash Memory Chip, Xianyang High-end Copper Foil Material, Yangling McCain Foods, and TaiKoo Li Culture and Commerce have been implemented successively. The newly established foreign-invested enterprises have increased by 29.9%, and the actual use of domestic capital has increased by 12.6%.

陕西秦龙良种奶山羊5G智慧产业园

特色产业
Specialty Industries

推进特色现代农业建设
Promoting Modern Agriculture with Distinctive Local Features

乡村振兴，产业兴旺是关键。陕西强化总体设计和政策供给，以"链长制"为抓手，集中打造苹果、茶叶、食用菌、乳制品、畜禽肉类、蔬菜、猕猴桃、中药材8条现代农业全

风景如画的汉中市宁强千山玉皇观茶园

产业链，陕西省农业农村厅研究出台特色产业发展《五年行动方案》，逐链条制定高质量发展意见，建立省部共建延安苹果，厅市共建柞水木耳、平利茶叶的工作

Industrial prosperity is the key to rural revitalization. With the focus on the "Chain Chief System", Shaanxi Province strengthened the overall design and policy supply to build eight modern agricultural whole industrial chains including apples, tea, edible fungi, dairy products, poultry and livestock meat, vegetables, kiwi fruit and Chinese herbs. The Department of Agriculture and Rural Affairs of Shaanxi Province issued a Five-Year Action Plan on the development of specialty industries and put forward suggestions on the high-quality development of each chain.

机制和政策框架。实施农产品加工增值提升行动和农业品牌精品培育计划，洛川苹果、米脂小米、眉县猕猴桃、韩城大红袍花椒4个区域公用品牌入选农业农村部农业品牌精品培育计划。2023年，陕西组织品牌营销活动200余场次，品牌影响力不断提升。通过一系列组合拳，实现巩固拓展脱贫攻坚成果和推进产业发展双赢，苹果、猕猴桃、羊奶产量均居全国首位，茶叶、食用菌产量和设施农业规模位居西北地区首位。

In addition, mechanisms and policy frameworks were established to support Yan'an Apple jointly built by the province and the state ministry, Zhashui agaric and Pingli Tea by the city and the provincial office.Actions were conducted in the added values of agricultural product processing and brand cultivation, Luochuan apple, Mizhi millet, Meixian County kiwifruit, and Hancheng Dahongpao peppercorns were selected by the Ministry of Agriculture and Rural Affairs into the excellent agricultural brand cultivation plan. In 2023, more than 200 brand marketing activities were organized by Shaanxi Province, enhancing their influence significantly. With the implementations of actions, a win-win achievement of consolidating and expanding the results of poverty alleviation and promoting industrial development has scored with the output of apples, kiwifruit, and goat's milk ranking the first across the country, and the output of tea, edible fungi, and the scale of facility-based agriculture ranking the first in the northwestern China.

中药生产车间的工人在选天麻片

子洲县何家集镇眠虎沟村的地头带货直播

文化旅游产业
Cultural and Tourism Industry

2023年，陕西文旅产业8条重点产业链营业收入7729.86亿元。全年接待省外游客1.09亿人次，同比增长271.94%。西安历史文化、延安红色旅游等特色产业群提质增效明显，演出服饰、毛绒玩具、秦巴生态康养等产业子群渐成规模。全年开工、投产文旅重点项目307个，总投资1569.6亿元，丝路欢乐世界、铜川花月荟等56个项目建成运营。17条线路入选文化和旅游

In 2023, the revenue from eight key industrial chains of Shaanxi's cultural and tourism industry achieved 772.986 billion yuan with annual reception of 109 million tourists from other provinces, a year-on-year increase of 271.94%. The quality and efficiency of specialty industry clusters such as Xi'an history and culture, Yan'an revolutionary tourism have been enhanced impressively. Other sub-clusters such as performance costumes, plush toys, Qinling-Daba ecological recuperation have been developing into scale. In addition, the cultural and tourism projects also enjoyed rapid development. For example, 307 key cultural and tourism projects were launched and put into production

灞河旁的西安文化地标性建筑——长安云

华清宫景区《长恨歌》演出

部"乡村四时好风光"精品线路,"革命圣地延安非遗之旅"入选全国非遗特色旅游线路,翠华山、玉华宫、照金、鳌山4个滑雪旅游点成功入选"古城千年·滑跃古今"全国十大冰雪旅游精品线路,文旅消费迸发新活力。

2024年,陕西将强化链群发展,壮大产业规模。积极推进重点文化旅游产业链群三年行动方案落实,力争年底实现营业总收入8500亿元。力争培育3家年接待游客1000万人次以上、5

with a total investment of 156.96 billion *yuan*, and 56 projects have been completed and put into operation such as the Silk Road Paradise and Tongchuan Flower Moon Tourist District. The culture and tourism consumption has unleashed new vitality. For example, 17 routes were selected as the Ministry of Culture and Tourism's "Beautiful Rural Scenery of Four Seasons" high-quality travel routes. The intangible cultural heritage journey to Yan'an—the sacred land of Chinese revolution was selected as the national travel to special cultural heritage. Mount Cuihua, Yuhua Palace, Zhaojin, Aoshan were selected into "Ancient and Modern Ski in Thousand-Year City" national top 10 ice and snow tourism routes.

In 2024, Shaanxi Province will enhance the chain clusters development and expand the industrial scale. Efforts

家年接待游客500万人次以上的旅游景区（街区）。培育做优特色民宿、文旅街区、沉浸体验、智慧旅游等新业态。支持做强数字演艺、动漫电竞等数字文旅优势产业，打造秦创原数字文旅产业平台和特色数字文旅产业园区基地，推动形成"一核多节点"的数字文旅产业布局。

will be made to vigorously promote the implementation of the three-year action plan for key cultural and tourism industrial chain clusters, strive to realize an income of 850 billion *yuan* by the end of the year, and foster three scenic sites or blocks which receive more than 10 million tourists per year and five ones which receive more than 5 million tourists per year. New forms of travel will be developed such as themed home stays, culture and tourism blocks, immersive experiences, and smart tourism. It is also imperative to support the digital tourism industries such as digital performing, animation and e-sports. The Qin Chuangyuan Digital Culture and Tourism Industry Platform and the Featured Digital Culture and Tourism Park Base are to be established, aiming to produce a digital tourism industrial layout with one core and multiple features.

宁陕县城关镇渔湾村的民宿干净整洁、环境宜人

大唐芙蓉园灯展

经济布局
Economic Layout

形成强劲推动力、支撑力
Generating Strong Impetus and Supporting Force

陕西围绕战略性新兴产业、未来产业重点优势领域，突出抓项目、促创新、强主体、优生态，探索形成"协同创新、链式整合、园区承载、集群带动"产业创新发展新路径，大幅提高全要素生产率，形成推动高质量发展的强劲推动力、支撑力。

Shaanxi focuses on key areas of strategic emerging industries and future industries, gives prominence to the project management, innovation, market entities, and ecological optimization. A new approach on industrial innovation and development has been put forward featuring collaborative innovation, chain integration, parks' carrying capacity and clusters' momentum. By doing so, the total-factor productivity has witnessed impressive improvement, creating a robust driving force for high-quality development.

加强关键核心技术攻关
Strengthening Breakthroughs in Core Technologies

陕西结合省内外相应领域科技基础条件，绘制创新链产业链深度对接耦合图谱，梳理形成关键核心技术需求清单和供给清单，双向对接、精准匹配，有组织地滚动实施科研计划项目，实行"揭榜挂帅""赛马制"等项目管理制度集中攻关，攻克一批关键核心技术，超前布局前沿未来技术和颠覆性技术，抢占产业竞争制高点。

Shaanxi formulates the framework on deep integration of innovation chain and industrial chain in line with the scientific and technological conditions in Shaanxi and other provinces. The demand and supply lists of core technologies have been sorted out so as to implement scientific research projects in a precise and organized manner. Science and technology reward project and knockout mechanism are rolled out to achieve breakthroughs in core technologies. In addition, forward-thinking plans for future and disruptive technologies are also drawn up to get in on the ground floor of industrial competitions.

西安迈科金属国际集团有限公司

提升协同创新水平
Enhancing Collaborative Innovation

陕西推进西安综合性国家科学中心和科技创新中心建设，发挥国家重大科技基础设施、陕西实验室体系作用，聚焦产业创新集群发展方向，高

Shaanxi efforts will be made to promote the construction of Xi'an Comprehensive National Center of Science and National Center of Technology Innovation, and to leverage the role of major national science and technology infrastructure and the Shaanxi laboratory system.

西安高新区

标准建设国家级和省级工程研究中心、产业创新中心、技术创新中心、制造业创新中心等创新平台，实施一批创新能力建设项目，持续推动产学研用协同创新，积极融入全球创新网络，把握产业发展主动权。

In addition, focusing on the development of industrial innovation clusters, we will establish national and provincial engineering research centers, industrial innovation centers, technological innovation centers, manufacturing innovation centers, and other innovation platforms with high standard. By implementing some innovation capacity-building projects, efforts will be made to continuously promote collaborative innovation between industry, education, research and application, actively integrate into the global innovation network, and seize the initiative in development.

强化企业科技创新主体地位
Strengthening the Dominant Position of Enterprises in Scientific and Technological Innovation

陕西加强以企业为主体的新型研发机构建设，推动产业创新集群领军企业牵头组建共性技术研发平台、创新联合体，加大技术研发、技术改造和提档升级力度。加强大中小企业协同创新，围绕全产业链协作和配套联合实施一批研发和成果转化项目，培育一批掌握自主核心技术、集成创新能力强的专精特新企业、瞪羚企业和独角兽企业。

Shaanxi will enhance the construction of new-type R&D institutions with enterprises as the primary force, encouraging leading enterprises in industrial innovation clusters to spearhead the establishment of common technology R&D platforms and innovation consortia. Additionally, we will increase efforts in technological research and development, technological transformation, and upgrading. We will also strengthen collaborative innovation among small, medium-sized, and large enterprises, focusing on collaborative implementation of a series of R&D and technology transfer projects across the entire industrial chain. Through this, we aim to cultivate a group of specialized, innovative, and technologically advanced enterprises, gazelle enterprises, and unicorn enterprises that possess independent core technologies and strong integrated innovation capabilities.

推进重大科技成果产业化
Promoting the Industrialization of Major Scientific and Technological Achievements

陕西建好用好秦创原平台，持续深化科技成果转化"三项改革"，完善科技成果转化服务体系。引导创新领军企业和专业机构建设一批中试基地项目，开展概念验证、中试熟化和小批量试生产。支持各市县、科研院所、高校建设专业化技术转移机构，实施一批重大科技成果产业化示范项目，积极推进重大技术装备示范应用，推动先进技术成果转化孵化产业化。

Shaanxi efforts will be exerted in promoting the industrialization of major scientific and technological achievements by effectively utilizing Qinchuangyuan Platform and continuously deepening the reforms in three aspects of labor, personnel and distribution concerning the transformation of scientific and technological achievements. We will enhance the service system for the transformation of scientific and technological achievements, encourage leading innovative enterprises and professional institutions to establish a number of pilot base projects, conduct concept verification, pilot maturation, and small-batch trial production. We will also support various cities and counties, research institutes, and universities in building specialized technology transfer institutions, implement a series of major scientific and technological achievements industrialization demonstration projects, actively promote the demonstration application of major technical equipment, and advance the transformation, incubation, and industrialization of advanced technological achievements.

黄龙县界头庙镇风车小镇

东方宝石
——朱鹮
Crested Ibis: Oriental Jewel

朱鹮，当今世界最濒危的鸟类之一，被世界自然保护联盟（IUCN）列入濒危物种名录。朱鹮也是中国特有物种，国家一级保护动物。有着"东方宝石"之称的朱鹮一度被认为已经灭绝，1981年5月，我国科学工作者在陕西洋县八里关乡姚家沟发现了数量仅为7只的朱鹮种群，在国内外引起轰动。"秦岭七君子"成为当时世界上唯一的野生朱鹮群，有着重要国际影响和特殊意义。

1986年，经陕西省人民政府批准，陕西朱鹮保护观察站成立，开始了有计划的保护和拯救工作。2001年，成立陕西朱鹮自然保护区。2005年7月，经国务院批准，成立陕西汉中朱鹮国家级自然保护区，面积37549公顷。这里成为世界珍禽朱鹮唯一的人工饲养种源地和主要野外栖息地，森林覆盖率达65.5%，被誉为地球上同纬度生态最好的地区之一。

目前，朱鹮的活动范围已由当时的洋县扩展到周边的汉中、安康、宝鸡、铜川4市15县，面积约1.4万平方千米，形成了"人与自然和谐共生"的生态局面，朱鹮已成为陕西一张亮丽的生态名片。

未来，陕西朱鹮保护区将借助"建立以国家公园为主体的自然保护地体系"的国家方略，持续推进自然资源的科学保护和合理利用，促进保护区与区域协调发展，让陕西生态文明建设迈向新时代。

As one of the world's most threatened ibis species, crested ibis is listed as an endangered animal on the IUCN Red List. As an endemic species in China, it is a first-grade state protection animal. Crested ibis, known as the "Oriental Jewel", was previously thought to be extinct in China until May 1981 when only seven ibises were seen in Yaojiagou, Baliguan Township of Yangxian County, Shaanxi, causing quite a stir both at home and abroad. At that time, Qinling Mountain Range became the only place with exiting wild ibises in the world which is of great international importance and special significance.

In 1986, under the approval of Shaanxi People's Government, Shaanxi Crested Ibis Observation Station was established for the bird's protection. Shaanxi Crested Ibis Nature Reserve was also founded in 2001. In addition, Shaanxi Hanzhong National Nature Reserve, with the approval of the State Council, was established in July 2005, with an area of 37,549 hm^2 and forestry coverage of 65.5%. It is the only reserve boasting captive and wild crested ibises in the world, known as one of the best ecological regions on the earth at the same latitude.

The distribution area of crested ibis has spread now from Yangxian County to 15 counties of four cities, including Hanzhong, Ankang, Baoji and Tongchuan, with a total of area of 14,000 square kilometers, reflecting the harmony between human beings and nature, enabling crested ibis an icon of ecology.

With the support of the national strategy of establishing park-oriented nature protection zones, Shaanxi Crested Ibis Nature Reserve will advance continuously the scientific protection and rational use of natural resources as well as the coordinated development of protection zones and the local area in the future, driving Shaanxi into a new stage in ecological civilization.

近年来，陕西以奋发有为的精神状态，把惠民生、暖民心、顺民意的工作做到群众心坎上，把政府对民生工作的决策部署变为可感可及的民生新图景。

In recent years, Shaanxi has been working diligently and proactively to benefit people's livelihood and satisfy their needs, turning the government's decisions on people's livelihood into a real and concrete one.

>

Chapter Four

第四篇

安居乐业，脱贫致富

丰年留客足鸡豚

Living and Working in Peace, Shaking off Poverty and Getting Rich

Ample Food for Guests in Good Years

便捷出行
Convenient Transportation

2023年，陕西省全年完成综合交通投资939.3亿元，同比增长14.9%，投资规模创近十年新高；高铁建设取得重大突破，推动延榆高铁当年立项、当年顺利开工，全省高铁建设总里程1010公里，

In 2023, the comprehensive transportation investment in Shaanxi Province has achieved 93.93 billion yuan, an increase of 14.9% year-on-year, hitting a new high in the past decade. The construction of high-speed railway has scored an impressive breakthrough with the Yan'an-Yulin High-speed Railway Project approved and launched in the same year. The high-speed rail network in Shaanxi Province stands at a total of over 1,010 kilometers, ranking among the top across the country and showing our accelerating efforts in high-speed railway construction. The structure of highway network enjoys sustained optimization, promoting

西安三桥立交

在建规模跻身全国第一方阵，跑出陕西高铁建设的"加速度"；公路网结构不断优化升级，综合枢纽城市集群加快成型，重大项目谋划接续有力。全年公路、水路客运量、铁路旅客发送量、机场旅客吞吐量，分别完成1.27亿人次、92万人次、1.2亿人次、4494万人次；公路、水路、铁路货运量、机场货邮吞吐量，分别达到13.4亿吨、51万吨、

the forming of a comprehensive hub city cluster and blueprinting great potential for major projects. In 2023, the passenger trips by highway, waterways, railway and the air hit over 127 million, 920,000, 120 million, and 44.94 million respectively; the corresponding ports achieved 1.34 billion tons, 510,000 tons, 330 million tons, and 280,000 tons respectively. The Xi'an Metro achieved 1.29 billion passenger trips. Efforts were also exerted to rural traffic with 9510 kilometers of newly-rebuilt and improved rural highways, 14 new townships with three-level highways, and 2560 natural villages with more than 30 households with access to paved roads. In addition, security projects of

西安咸阳国际机场一角

3.3亿吨、28万吨。西安地铁完成客运量12.9亿人次。新改建完善农村公路9510公里，新增通三级公路乡镇14个，新增通硬化路30户以上自然村2560个。实施农村公路安防工程4259公里，改造农村公路危桥157座。累计创建"四好农村路"省级示范市5个、示范县78个，"四好农村路"发展进入新阶段，城乡交通运输一体化发展水平达到5A级，交通助农惠农有力有效。

4259 kilometers of rural roads were completed and 157 dangerous bridges on rural highway have been renovated. Thanks to these efforts, the "Four Good Rural Road" which refers to a sound improvement of construction, management, maintenance and operation of roads in rural areas have seen significant achievement with five provincial demonstration cities and 78 demonstration counties. The integration of urban and rural transportation has reached AAAAA−level, bringing great and effective benefits to agriculture, rural areas and farmers.

动车组列车驶入西安北站

民生工程
Livelihood Projects

教育
Education

2023年，陕西加强优质教育资源均衡供给，投入35.1亿元改善1646所义务教育学校办学条件。高等教育第

In 2023, Shaanxi strengthened the balanced supply of quality education resources, investing 3.51 billion yuan in improving the conditions of 1646 compulsory education schools. Disciplines ranking the first level

西安交通大学创新港校区

西安航天城第一幼儿园老师给小朋友讲授科普知识

三方评估第一层次学科增长89%，国家级教学成果获奖数全国第三，高校承担企事业单位委托经费（理工农医类）全国第四。

in the higher education evaluation initiated by the third party increased by 89%, with the number of national teaching achievement awards ranking the third, and funds entrusted on colleges and universities by enterprises and institutes in the fields of science, technology, agriculture and medicine ranking the fourth in the whole country.

医疗
Medical Care

2023年,陕西持续深化综合医改,西安交大一附院榆林医院获批建设国家区域医疗中心,83个县启动建设紧密型县域医共体。

医疗构型直升机落地唐都医院

In 2023, efforts were also made to continuously deepen comprehensive medical reform with Yulin Hospital, the First Affiliated Hospital of Xi'an Jiaotong University approved to build the national regional medical center and close county medical communities being built in 83 counties.

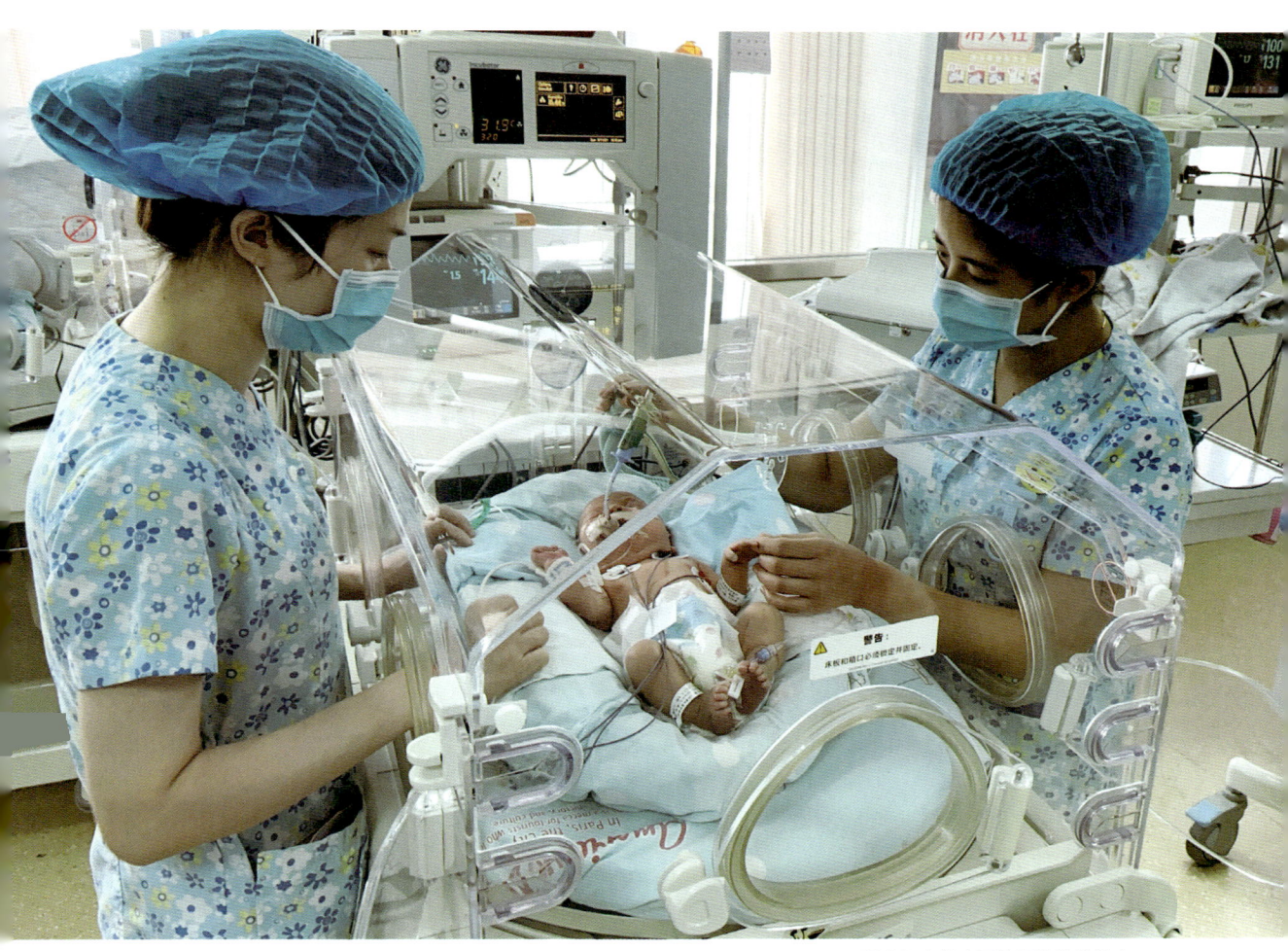

西北妇女儿童医院新生儿监护室

就业
Employment

2023年,陕西开展就业创业十大行动,发放稳岗资金9.2亿元、创业担保贷款63亿元,城镇新增就业43万人,全省居民人均可支配收入增长6.7%。

In 2023, Shaanxi rolled out ten major actions on employment and entrepreneurship, releasing 920 million *yuan* to stabilize employments and 6.3 billion *yuan* of start-up loans, offering new urban jobs to 430,000 people and the per capita residents' disposable income increasing by 6.7 % in the province.

陕西北人印刷机械有限责任公司零部件成套中心内,工人在装配机器

咸阳市永寿县绿菜公司开发岗位吸纳村民就业

公共文化服务
Public Cultural Service

2023年，为促进文化事业繁荣发展，陕西承办首届亚洲文化遗产保护联盟大会、第四届中国考古学大会，举办第十届陕西省艺术节、孙思邈中医药文化节，古树名木保护全面加强，延安革命文物国家文物保护利用示范区建成，旬邑西头遗址入选"全国十大考古新发现"，陕西历史博物馆秦汉馆、黄河文化博物馆、石峁博物馆建成开放，话剧《路遥》等5部作品入选新时代舞台艺术优秀剧目，陕北民歌音乐会全国巡演成功，《长恨歌》《驼铃传奇》《无界·长安》《延安保育院》等一批演艺精品市场火热。

To promote the prosperous development of cultural undertakings, we successfully held the First General Assembly of the Alliance for Cultural Heritage in Asia, the Fourth Congress of Chinese Archeology, the Tenth Shaanxi Provincial Arts Festival, and Sun Simiao Traditional Chinese Medicine Culture Festival in 2023. Efforts were also pledged to protect ancient and famous trees. National Demonstration Area of National Cultural Relics Protection and Utilization of Yan'an Revolutionary Cultural Relics was built. Xitou Ruins in Xunyi County of Shaanxi Province was selected into national top 10 new discoveries. The Qin Han Museum of the Shaanxi History Museum, Shaanxi Yellow River Culture Museum and Shimao Museum have been built and opened to public. The drama "Lu Yao" and five other works were selected as the outstanding stage plays in the new era. The Northern Shaanxi Folk Song Concert successfully finished its tour show around the country, and a number of performing arts hit the market, including "Chang Hen Ge", "Camel Bell Legend", "Boundless Chang'an", and "Yan'an Nursery".

安康市白河县共享图书馆

曲江新开门运动公园

乡村振兴
Rural Revitalization

发展壮大县域经济
Developing and Boosting the County Economy

2023年，面对复杂严峻的内外部环境，全省上下深入贯彻落实县域经济高质量发展大会精神，完

In 2023, facing the complex and severe domestic and international environment, Shaanxi Province further implemented the spirit of the conference on high quality development of county economy, and perfected the

棣花古镇千亩荷塘

善推动县域经济高质量发展体制机制，围绕主导产业培育和特色发展，以"一县一策"为重要抓手，有效

system and mechanism for promoting its high-quality development. Withe the focus on the cultivation of leading industries and characteristic development, we took "one county, one policy" as an important lever to

推动全省县域经济稳步发展。2023年全省县域83个县（市、区）地区生产总值16205.40亿元，按不变价计算，较上年增长4.0%，占全省地区生产总值的比重48.0%，县域经济发展基础夯实加固，高质量发展稳步推进。

effectively promote steady development of county economy throughout the province. 2023 witnessed 1620.54 billion *yuan* of the gross domestic product of 83 counties (cities, districts) in Shaanxi Province, an increase of 4.0% compared to the previous year at constant prices, accounting for 48.0% of the province's regional gross domestic product, providing consolidated and strengthened foundation for county-level economic development and steady advancement of high-quality development.

咸阳市淳化县十里塬镇整齐的村舍

杨凌示范区金鹏种业公司内,工作人员在采摘用于育种的西红柿

促进乡村宜居宜业
Promoting Livable and Workable Rural Areas

2023年,陕西省启动实施"千村示范、万村提升"工程,不断巩固拓展脱贫攻坚成果,脱贫人口人均纯收入增长15.2%,持续强化宜居宜业和美乡村建设,乡村振兴相关具体工作取得新的进展。

In 2023, the "Thousand Villages Demonstration, Ten Thousand Villages Renovation" project was launched in Shaanxi, and sustained efforts were exerted in consolidating and expanding the achievements of poverty alleviation, and the construction of livable and workable beautiful rural areas, with the per capita net income of the poverty-stricken population increasing by 15.2%, generating new progress in specific work related to rural revitalization.

促进农民富裕富足
Promoting Affluence among Farmers

陕西加强农业全产业链建设，聚焦延链、强链、补链，发展壮大延安苹果、柞水木耳、平利茶叶等优势特色产业，着力推广科技助农型产业、劳动密集型产业、高质量庭院经济、农文旅融合发展"四种模式"，加强帮扶产业联农带农情况监测。

Shaanxi strengthened the construction of the entire agricultural industry chain, focusing on extending, strengthening, and supplementing the chain, developing advantageous characteristic industries such as Yan'an apples, Zhashui agaric, and Pingli tea. Efforts were made to promote the "four models" of technology assisted agriculture, labor-intensive industries, high-quality courtyard economy, and integrated development of agriculture, culture, and tourism, and to strengthen the monitoring of the situation of industry assisted agriculture.

荷兰客商盛赞洛川苹果

小木耳大产业

秦东沃野，关中粮仓
——关中平原
Guanzhong Plain: A Fertile Land in Eastern Shaanxi and the Granary of Guanzhong

关中平原是陕西省秦岭北麓的渭河冲积平原，亦称渭河平原，平均海拔约500米，位于关中盆地的中部、晋陕盆地带的南部。其北部为陕北黄土高原，向南则是秦巴山脉，西起宝鸡，东至渭南。关中平原乃陕西的富庶之地，也是人口密集地区，工、农业发达，号称"八百里秦川"。

渭河由西向东横贯关中平原，其干流及支流泾河、北洛河等均有灌溉之利，中国古

Guanzhong Plain, also called the Weihe Plain, is an alluvial plain of the Weihe River at the northern foot of Qinling Mountain Range in Shaanxi Province. It is at an average elevation of about 500 meters, located in the central part of the Guanzhong Basin and the southern part of the Jin-Shaan Basin. To the north of Guanzhong Plain is Shaanbei Loess Plateau, and to its south is the Qinling-Daba Mountain Range. Extending from Baoji in the west to Weinan in the east, Guanzhong Plain is an affluent place in Shaanxi with a dense population and developed industries and agriculture, known as "800-li Qinchuan".

The Weihe River runs through Guanzhong Plain from west to east, and its main stream and tributaries, the Jinghe River and the Beiluo River, are

富平县流曲镇吉顺祥家庭农场金黄色的麦田

代著名水利工程如郑国渠、白渠、漕渠、成国渠、龙首渠都引自这些河流。关中平原自然、经济条件优越,是中国历史上农业最富庶地区之一,有"关中粮仓"之称。

"天府"是说某地物产丰饶,犹如天之库府。最早被称为"天府"的是关中。战国时期,苏秦向秦惠王陈说"连横"之计时,称颂关中"田肥美,民殷富,战车万乘,奋击百贸,沃野千里,蓄积多饶",并说"此所谓天府,天下之雄国也",这比四川盆地获得"天府之国"的称谓早了500多年。这是因为关中从战国郑国渠修好以后,就成了物产丰富、帝王建都的风水宝地。

all beneficial for irrigation. In addition, some famous water conservation projects in ancient China such as the Zhengguo Canal, the Bai Canal, the Cao Canal, the Chengguo Canal and the Longshou Canal are all drawn from these rivers. As one of the most affluent agricultural regions in Chinese history, Guanzhong Plain boasts superior natural resources and economic conditions, reputed as the "Guanzhong Granary."

The "Land of Abundance" refers to the area enjoying rich resources, like the treasury of Heaven. Guanzhong was the first place to be acclaimed as "the Land of Abundance". During the Warring States period, Su Qin recommended the strategy of alliance to the King of Qinhui, and praised Guanzhong as enjoying "a fertile land with tens and thousands of chariots, millions of best soldiers, a vast land full of abundant resources, and people here living a prosperous life", claiming here as "the Land of Abundance, a powerful country in the world." Guanzhong has enjoyed the reputation of "Land of Abundance" over 500 years earlier than Sichuan Basin. This is because that since the period of Warring States, after the construction of Zhengguo Canal, Guanzhong has been a prosperous land for the emperors to build capitals.

陕西是闻名世界的古丝绸之路起点，也是"一带一路"的重要节点，区位优势独特、创新动能强劲、开放优势明显、营商环境优越。近年来，陕西利用自身区位优势，以共建"一带一路"为引领，不断推动陕西外向型经济高质量发展。

Shaanxi is the starting point of the world-famous ancient Silk Road and a vital node in the development of the Belt and Road Initiative. Moreover, Shaanxi enjoys unique location advantages, strong innovative power, obvious advantages in opening-up, and an excellent business environment.

〉

Chapter Five

第五篇

海纳百川，兼容并包

百川衮衮东赴海

Embracing and All-inclusive

All Rivers Flowing East to the Sea

融入"一带一路"
Response to the "Belt and Road Initiative"

党的二十大报告指出,"共建'一带一路'成为深受欢迎的国际公共产品和国际合作平台",并提出了"推动共建'一带一路'高质量发展"的要求。共建"一带一路"倡议提出以来,我国始终坚持共商共建共享原则,以高标准、可持续、惠民生为目标,聚焦重点领域、重点地区、重点项目,持续推进民生工程、民心工程,为推动构建人类命运共同体、畅通国内国际双循环提供了有力支撑和强劲动力。

2023年是共建"一带一路"倡议提出十周年,陕西积极落实习近平总书记关于共建"一带一路"重要论述和历次来陕考察重要讲话重要指示,持续放大中国—中亚峰会效应,扎实推进"一带一路"五大中心建设,各项工作取得积极进展。

The report of the Party's 20th National Congress pointed out that "the development of the Belt and Road Initiative has become a popular international public goods and cooperation platform", and also put forward the requirements of "promoting the high-quality development of the Belt and Road Initiative". Since the joint development of the Belt and Road Initiative was put forward, we have been adhering to the principle of extensive consultation, joint contribution and shared benefits. Guided by the goal of high standards, sustainable development and people's livelihood benefit, we focus on key areas, key zones and key projects and continuously promote projects beneficial to the people and those in the interest of the public, so as to provide strong support and impetus for promoting the building of a community with a shared future for mankind and smoothing domestic and international dual circulation.

2023 marked the tenth anniversary of the proposal of the Belt and Road Initiative. Shaanxi actively implemented General Secretary Xi Jinping's important speech on jointly building the Belt and Road and his important instructions during inspections in Shaanxi, continued to amplify the effects of the China-Central Asia Summit, and solidly advanced the construction of the five centers of the Belt and Road Initiative, with all tasks making positive progress.

第七届丝绸之路国际博览会暨中国东西部合作与投资贸易洽谈会在西安开幕

中欧班列深度融入"一带一路"大格局

中欧班列（西安）持续领跑全国
China-Europe Railway Express (Xi'an) Continuing to Lead in the Nation

2023年，中欧班列（西安）常态化运行17条国际线路，与哈铁合作推出西安—巴库跨里海运输线路，深度融入西部陆海新通道，全年开行5351列，同比增长15.3%，是全国增幅的2倍以上，开行量、货运量、重箱率等核心指标稳居全国第一，西安成为全国首个年度开行超5000列、累计开行超2万列的城市。在全国率先实现"港区联动、抵港直装"、海关铁路数据联通、稳定开行往返境内外全程时刻表中欧班列，对地方经济带动不断增强。

In 2023, the China-Europe Railway Express (Xi'an) operated 17 regular international routes, launched the Xi'an-Baku Caspian Sea transportation route in cooperation with Kazakhstan Railways, and further integrated into the new western land-sea corridor. A total of 5,351 trips were operated throughout the year, a year-on-year increase of 15.3%, more than double the national growth rate. Core indicators such as the number of trains operated, cargo volume, and load factor ranked first in the country. Xi'an became the first city in the country to operate over 5,000 trains annually and a cumulative total of over 20,000 trains. It took the lead nationally in realizing "port area linkage, direct loading at the port", interconnectivity of customs and railway data, and stable operation of China-Europe Railway Express trains with full schedules to and from domestic and international destinations, continuously enhancing the economic impact on the local economy.

与共建"一带一路"国家贸易额累计超万亿元
Trade Volume with Belt and Road Initiative Countries Surpassing Trillion *Yuan*

2013—2023年,陕西对共建"一带一路"国家累计进出口值13339亿元,年度进出口总值由2013年的416.6亿元,增加到2023年的2099.3亿元,年均增长17.6%。陕汽集团在15个共建国家建成了本地化工厂,产品远销140多个国家和地区。法士特成功加

From 2013 to 2023, Shaanxi's total import and export volume with countries involved in the Belt and Road Initiative reached 13.339 trillion *yuan*. The annual total volume of imports and exports increased from 41.66 billion *yuan* in 2013 to 209.93 billion *yuan* in 2023, with an average annual growth rate of 17.6%. Shaanxi Automobile Group has established localized factories in 15 participating

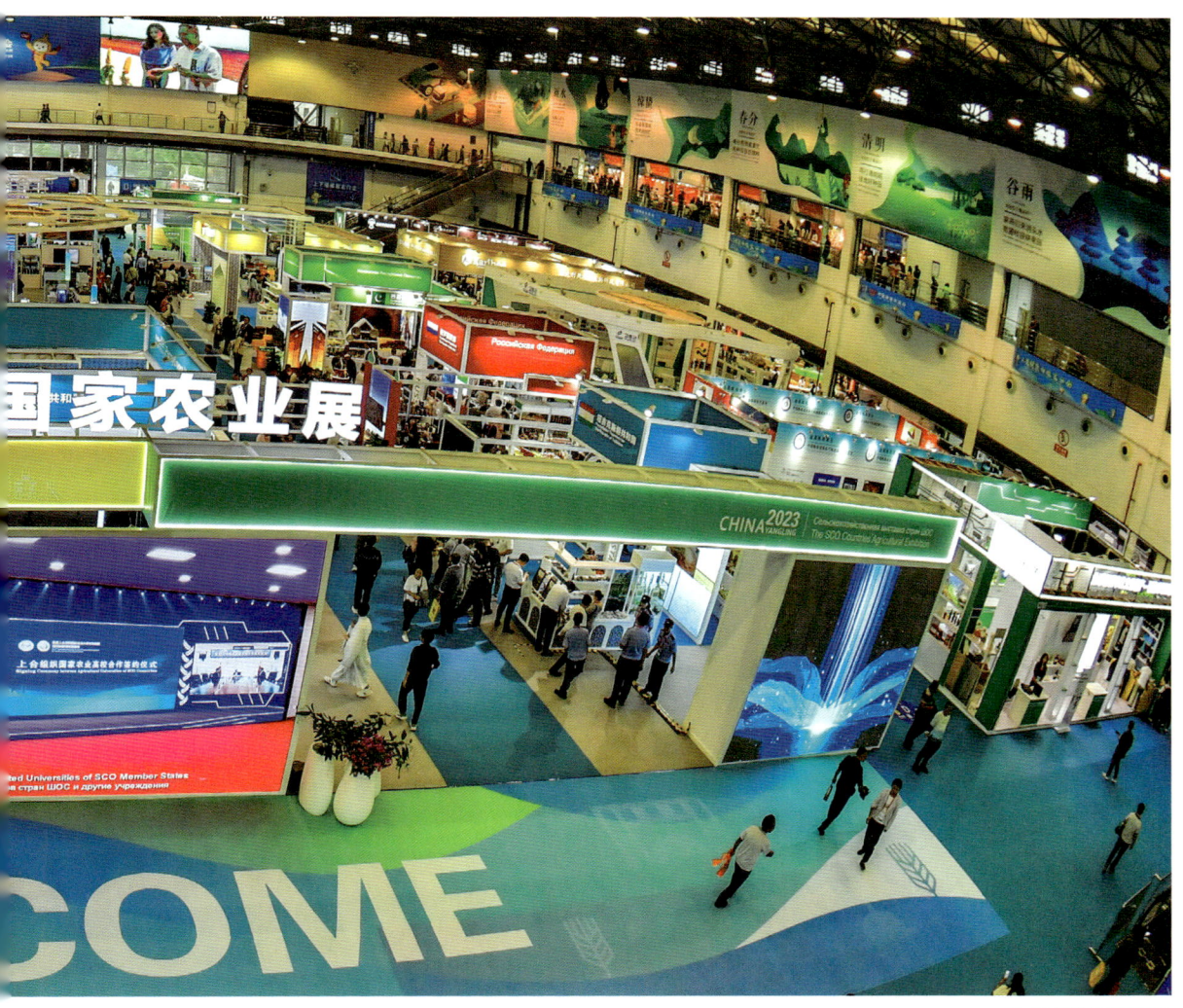

第30届杨凌农高会

入戴姆勒等世界著名汽车及零部件企业全球供应链体系，广泛出口50多个国家和地区。爱菊粮油建成"三位一体"跨国大物流大加工体系，"一带一路"供应链模式入选国家首批新型消费发展典型案例。

countries, with products exported to more than 140 countries and regions. Fast Gear successfully joined the global supply chain systems of world-renowned automobile and parts companies like Daimler, exporting widely to over 50 countries and regions. Aiju Grain and Oil has built a "trilateral" transnational logistics and processing system, with its Belt and Road supply chain model selected as one of the country's first batch of new consumer development cases.

与共建"一带一路"国家资金融通迈上新台阶
Financial Integration with Belt and Road Initiative Countries Reaching New Heights

2023年，陕西实现跨境人民币收付近千亿元，创历史新高，增速排名全国第十。跨境人民币优质企业数量达373家，同比增长145.39%。与中亚五国人民币跨境收付14.54亿元，同比增长209.15%；与83个共建国家人民币跨境收付397.74亿元，同比增长113.83%，增速排名全国第三。跨境人民币累计结算额5397.21亿元，服务企业5503家，实现"双突破"。

In 2023, Shaanxi achieved nearly 100 billion *yuan* in cross-border Renminbi payments and receipts, setting a new historical record and ranking tenth nationally. The number of high-quality cross-border Renminbi enterprises reached 373, a year-on-year increase of 145.39%. Cross-border Renminbi payments and receipts with the five Central Asian countries amounted to 1.454 billion *yuan*, a year-on-year increase of 209.15%, and 39.774 billion yuan with 83 Belt and Road countries, a year-on-year increase of 113.83%, ranking third nationally. Cross-border Renminbi cumulative settlement amounted to 539.721 billion *yuan*, serving 5,503 companies and achieving a "dual breakthrough."

跨境人民币结算体系助力对外贸易

涉外法治服务体系为境外企业"走进来"、国内企业"走出去"提供坚实的法律保障

涉外法治服务持续优化
Continuous Optimization of Foreign-Related Legal Services

陕西全面加强"一带一路"的检察保护，最高检"一带一路"检察研究基地在西安落户，中国—中亚法律查明与研究中心建成并运行，设立"一带一路"检察服务中心，圆满承办第21次上合组织成员国总检察长会议，成功举办越南高级检察官来华研修班。加强同最高法第六巡回法庭、第二国际商事法庭协作，推广"调解—仲裁—行政裁决—诉讼"多元化解方式，十年来审结的各类涉外商事及仲裁司法审查案件，涵盖跨境生产、贸易、金融等多个领域，覆盖欧亚非30多个国家和地区，辐射新加坡、伊朗、塔吉克斯坦、俄罗斯等共建国家。

Shaanxi has comprehensively strengthened prosecutorial protection for the Belt and Road Initiative. The Supreme People's Procuratorate's Belt and Road prosecutorial Research Base was established in Xi'an, and the China-Central Asia Legal Identification and Research Center was built and put into operation. A Belt and Road prosecutorial service center was set up, successfully hosting the 21st meeting of the Prosecutors-General of the Shanghai Cooperation Organization member states and organizing a training class in China for senior Vietnamese prosecutors. Collaboration was strengthened with the Supreme Court's Sixth Circuit Court and the Second International Commercial Court, promoting the "mediation-arbitration-administrative adjudication-litigation" diversified dispute resolution methods. Over the past decade, more than 8,000 cases of foreign-related commercial and arbitration judicial reviews have been concluded, covering cross-border production, trade, finance, and other fields, affecting over 30 countries and regions across Europe, Asia, and Africa, and impacting Belt and Road countries such as Singapore, Iran, Tajikistan, and Russia.

成功举行中国—中亚峰会
Successfully Hosting the China-Central Asia Summit

西安街头布置起"西安欢迎您"景观迎接中国—中亚峰会

2023年5月18日至19日，在国家主席习近平主持下，中国—中亚峰会成功在西安举行，这是中国同中亚国家建交31年来首次以实体形式举办峰会，是中国—中亚机

From May 18th to 19th, 2023, under the chairmanship of President Xi Jinping, the China-Central Asia Summit was successfully held in Xi'an, marking the first time that a summit was held in a physical format in the 31 years since the establishment

制建立3年来的首次峰会，向世界展示了中国方案、中国精神、中国力量，在中国—中亚关系史上树立起一座新的历史丰碑，在我国对外交往史上写下了浓墨重彩的篇章。峰会对中国—中亚机制进行了全面布局，正式建立元首会晤机制，设立常设秘书处，达成《西安宣言》《成果清单》等7份双多边文件，签署了100余份各领域合作协议，成果之丰、内容之实、影响之大前所未有。

陕西省委、省政府主要领导分别率代表团赴中亚对接落实峰会涉陕成果，形成系列访问成果，110条清单事项有序推进，哈萨克斯坦驻西安总领事馆开馆，哈萨克斯坦西安码头建成投用，实现中亚"五国六城"通航全覆盖。2023年，陕西与中亚五国实现进出口57.9亿元，同比增长178%。

of diplomatic relations between China and Central Asian countries. It was also the first summit since the establishment of the China-Central Asia Mechanism three years ago, showcasing to the world China's proposals, spirit, and strength. This event has erected a new historic milestone in the history of China-Central Asia relations and has inscribed a vivid and significant chapter in the history of China's foreign interactions. The summit has made a comprehensive layout of the China-Central Asia Mechanism, formally established the meeting mechanism of the heads of states, set up a permanent secretariat, reached seven bilateral and multilateral documents including the "Xi'an Declaration" and "Outcome List". Additionally, over 100 cooperation agreements were signed in various fields. The results were unprecedented in terms of their abundance, content, and influence.

Shaanxi delegations, led by the main leaders of the Shaanxi Provincial Party Committee and the Provincial Government, visited Central Asian countries to implement the Shaanxi-related outcomes of the summit, and have achieved a series of results. The 110 list items were orderly promoted, together with the opening of the Kazakhstan Consulate General in Xi'an, the completion and operation of the Kazakhstan Xi'an dock, realizing the full coverage of navigation in the "five countries and six cities" in Central Asia. 2023 witnessed an import and export volume of 5.79 billion yuan between Shaanxi and the five Central Asian countries, a year-on-year increase of 178%.

自贸区建设
Free Trade Zone Construction

陕西自贸试验区自 2017 年 4 月揭牌运行以来，围绕战略定位和发展目标深入开展制度创新，有效融入和服务国家重大战略，对全省深化改革、扩大开放发挥了引领示范作用。

Since its launch in April 2017, Shaanxi Pilot Free Trade Zone has carried out in-depth institutional innovation by centering on its strategic positioning and development goals. Effectively integrating and serving major national strategies, it has played a leading and exemplary role in deepening reform and opening wider to the outside world in Shaanxi Province.

In recent years, Shaanxi Pilot Free Trade Zone has given full play to its location advantages, and has continuously improved

中俄丝路创新园

近年来，陕西自贸试验区充分发挥自身区位优势，通过优化作业流程、创新监管模式和强化服务保障等通关便利化系统集成改革创新，不断提升通关效率、降低物流成本、优化通关服务，着力构筑内陆地区效率高、成本低、服务优的国际贸易通道，更加主动融入和服务构建新发展格局，更加深度融入共建"一带一路"大格局。

customs clearance efficiency, reduced logistics costs, optimized customs clearance services, and striven to build a customs clearance system through optimizing operating procedures, innovating supervision models, and strengthening service guarantees. In addition, great efforts were exerted to build an international trade channel with high efficiency, low cost and excellent service in inland areas, take more initiative in integrating into and serving the construction of a new development pattern, and further merge into the overall pattern of jointly building the the Belt and Road Initiative.

提升制度型开放水平
Improving Institutional Opening up

陕西发挥自贸试验区先行示范作用，对标高标准国际经贸规则，在知识产权、数字贸易等领域开展探索，在具有陕西特色的种业、医疗、教育、旅游、文化等领域加大开放力度，稳步推进规则、规制、管理、标准等制度型开放，不断构建与国际通行规则相衔接的制度体系。

We will give full play to the pioneering and demonstration role of Shaanxi Pilot Free Trade Zone. Under the guidance of high-standard international economic and trade rules, we will carry out exploration in areas such as intellectual property rights and digital trade, and open our door even wider in areas with the Shaanxi characteristics including seed industry, medical treatment, education, tourism and culture. We will steadily promote institutional opening up in rules, regulations, governance and standards, and continuously build an institutional system that is in line with international norms.

中国（陕西）自由贸易试验区

法士特高智新工厂简仓

提升制度创新能级
Upgrading the System Innovation

陕西深化首创性、集成化、差别化改革探索，在促进国内外人才、资本、技术、数据等要素自由流动方面加大探索力度；聚焦战略定位，积极打造中欧班列（西安）集结中心、西安航空枢纽，深入推进面向中亚、南亚、西亚的国际贸易通道、商贸物流枢纽、重要产业和人文交流基地的"丝路自贸"建设；发挥陕西省科教资源优势，突出科技创新、科技成果转化、创新链发展探索，加强国际交流，深入推进"科创自贸""农业自贸"建设，形成片区、功能区各具特色的探索路径，构建"一带一路"高标准自由贸易园区，积极开展赋权研究，推动下放更多省级经济管理权限，争取更多中央事权在陕西自贸试验区进行先行先试。

We will deepen the exploration of original, integrated and differentiated reform and put more efforts into the promotion of the free flow of talent, capital, technology, data and other factors at home and abroad. We will focus on strategic positioning and actively build an assembly center for China-Europe Railway Express and an aviation hub in Xi'an. We will also further promote the construction of the "Silk Road Free Trade" as an international trade corridor, commercial logistics hub, and key industrial and cultural exchange base for Central Asia, South Asia and West Asia. We will give full play to the advantages of scientific and educational resources in Shaanxi Province, highlighting scientific and technological innovation, achievement transformation in science and technology, and exploration of innovation chain development. We will also strengthen international exchanges, fully promote the construction of "Science and Innovation Free Trade" and "Agriculture Free Trade", so as to form a distinctive exploration path for each of the zones and functional areas. We will construct a high-standard free trade zone along the "Belt and Road Initiative", actively carry out research on empowerment, promote the devolution of more provincial-level economic management authority, and strive for more central authority in the Shaanxi Pilot Free Trade Zone for early and pilot implementation.

提升产业聚集的规模和质量
Enhancing the Scale and Quality of Industrial Clusters

陕西以制度创新赋能产业聚集发展，着力引导进出口企业、重要外资项目更多地在自贸试验区布局，强化主导产业在全国的优势地位，支持新业态新模式在自贸试验区发展，推动自贸试验区外向型经济发展，进一步打造内陆改革开放高地。

We will empower the industrial clusters with institutional innovation, focus on guiding more import and export enterprises and important foreign-funded projects to be located in the Pilot Free Trade Zone, and further strengthen the dominant position of leading industries in the country. We will support the development of new business operations and models in the Pilot Free Trade Zone, promoting the export-oriented economic development of the zone, and further building a highland for inland reform and opening up.

秦创原总窗口西咸新区一角

提升开放平台融合发展水平
Enhancing the Integrated Development of Open Platforms

陕西发挥自贸试验区先行先试和制度创新优势，统筹推动开发区、综保区、跨境电商综试区、进口贸易促进创新示范区、服务贸易基地等各类功能性、服务性开放平台功能优化整合，健全体制机制，用好用足政策，以开放平台聚资源、谋创新、促发展。

Exerting the advantages of the institutional innovation and the Pilot Free Trade Zone, we will coordinate the optimized integration of various functional and service-based open platforms such as development zones, comprehensive bonded zones, cross-border e-commerce integrated experimental areas, import trade promotion and innovation demonstration zones and service trade bases. We will pay more efforts in improving the institutional mechanism, making good use of policies, and using the open platform to gather resources, seek innovation and promote better development.

国际交流合作
International Exchange and Cooperation

成功举办首届亚洲文化遗产保护联盟大会
The First General Assembly of the Alliance for Cultural Heritage in Asia Successfully Held

陕西成功举办首届亚洲文化遗产保护联盟大会，亚洲21个国家和3个国际组织共150位代表参会，丝绸之路考古合作研究中心揭牌，《亚洲文化遗产保护联盟西安宣言》发布。中国—中亚峰会期间迎宾仪式、非遗项目展示等文化活动亮点纷呈，展现了"中国气派、陕西风采"，得到党和国家领导人、与会各国元首的高度赞誉。赴中亚3国开展11场文旅交流活动，成功举办陕西与中亚国家文艺交流会演，圆满承办土库曼斯坦中国文化年开幕式，实现了陕西与中亚国家人文交流满怀诚意的"双向奔赴"。

Shaanxi successfully held the first General Assembly of the Alliance for Cultural Heritage in Asia. A total of 150 representatives from 21 Asian countries and three international organizations attended the conference. The Cooperative Research Center for Archaeology of the Silk Road was unveiled and the "Xi'an Declaration of the Alliance for Cultural Heritage in Asia" was released. During the China–Central Asia Summit, cultural activities such as the welcoming ceremony and the display of intangible cultural heritage items were highlighted, which showed the "Chinese style and Shaanxi style", and were highly praised by the Party and state leaders and heads of states attending the summit. We went to three Central Asian countries to carry out 11 cultural and tourism exchange activities, successfully held a cultural exchange performance between Shaanxi and Central Asian countries, and hosted the opening ceremony of the Chinese Culture Year in Turkmenistan, realizing a sincere "two-way effort" for cultural exchanges between Shaanxi and Central Asian countries.

第十届中国西部文化产业博览会上，哈萨克斯坦展馆的工作人员给观众介绍旅游线路

农业对外交流合作丰富多元
Rich and Diversified International Exchange and Cooperation in Agriculture

陕西全力推进中国—中亚旱区农业"一带一路"联合实验室（国家级）创建工作，中哈草食家畜资源创新国际联合实验室、中哈动物科学国际联合实验室顺利揭牌。与吉尔吉斯斯坦楚河州、俄罗斯新西伯利亚州等地方省州合作共建的境外农业合作园区启动建设。成功承办上合组织减贫和可持续发展论坛、首届中国—中亚农业部长会、全球土壤健康论坛等国家主场外事活动。上合组织农业基地正式获批加入上合组织睦邻友好合作委员会，2023年以来，共培训 700 多名共建国家农业官员、技术人员。

Shaanxi has made every effort to promote the establishment of the China-Central Asia Arid Area Agriculture "Belt and Road" Joint Laboratory (national level). The China-Kazakhstan International Joint Laboratory for Herbivorous Livestock Resources Innovation and the China-Kazakhstan International Joint Laboratory for Animal Science were successfully inaugurated. The construction of overseas agricultural cooperation parks jointly built with Kyrgyzstan's Chuhe Oblast and Russia's Novosibirsk Oblast and other local provinces and states has been launched. Shaanxi has successfully hosted the SCO Poverty Reduction and Sustainable Development Forum, the First China-Central Asia Agriculture Ministers' Meeting, the Global Soil Health Forum and other national foreign affairs events. The SCO Agricultural Base has been officially approved to join the SCO Good-Neighborliness, Friendship and Cooperation Commission. Since 2023, more than 700 agricultural officials and technical personnel in the co-building countries have received training here.

杨凌小麦新品种在哈萨克斯坦"中哈"现代农业创新示范园获得丰收

教育国际合作影响力持续提升
Increasing Influence of International Education Cooperation

"丝绸之路大学联盟"启动"中国—中亚高等教育合作机制",新增10所中亚高校,在塔什干信息技术大学揭牌成立"西安交通大学乌兹别克斯坦创新中心",与撒马尔罕国立大学共建的"中国中心"揭牌,已有38个国家和地区的170所高校成为联盟成员;"一带一路"职教联盟已有来自17个国家的113所职业院校、行业协会、企业加入,"丝绸之路农业教育科技创新联盟"已有18个国家的96所涉农高校及研究机构入盟。成功举办2023丝绸之路教育合作交流会和2023丝绸之路国际产学研用合作会议,共促成合作项目28项。办好自主品牌"秦岭工坊",为共建国家培养适应国际市场的职业技能人才,累计在欧亚非三大洲7国设立7个"秦岭工坊"。

The "University Alliance of the Silk Road" launched the "China-Central Asia Higher Education Cooperation Mechanism", adding 10 more Central Asian universities. The "Xi'an Jiaotong University – Uzbekistan Innovation Center" at the Tashkent University of Information Technology was established, and the "China Centre" jointly established with Samarkand State University was inaugurated, with 170 universities from 38 countries and regions becoming members of the alliance. The "Belt and Road" Vocational Education Alliance boasts 113 vocational schools, industry associations, and enterprises from 17 countries. 96 agricultural-related universities and research institutions from 18 countries has joined the "Silk Road Agricultural Education and Research Innovation Alliance". The 2023 Silk Road Education Cooperation Expo and the 2023 Silk Road International Conference on the Cooperation and Integration of Industry, Education, Research, and Application were successfully held, and a total of 28 cooperation projects were promoted. Efforts were exerted in managing Shaanxi brand "Qinling Workshop" and cultivating vocational talents geared to the international market for the jointly built countries, with a total of seven "Qinling Workshops" established in seven countries in Europe, Asia and Africa.

艺术家用中国和吉尔吉斯斯坦传统纹饰元素创作的作品《丝路同欣》

陕西国际传播中心成立仪式

成立陕西国际传播中心
Establishment of Shaanxi International Communication Center

陕西为加强国际传播能力建设，推动文明交流互鉴，成立陕西国际传播中心，搭建起具有陕西特色的对外传播平台。该中心以共建"一带一路"倡议十周年为契机，全方位展现陕西服务国家对外开放大局所取得的亮点与成效。组织召开十周年系列新闻发布会，编制出版《陕西推进"一带一路"建设蓝皮书（2013—2023）》，并于第七届丝博会期间举办共建"一带一路"十周年成果展、中欧班列西安集结中心高质量发展论坛，面向世界讲好陕西故事、丝路故事。

In order to strengthen the construction of international communication capabilities and promote exchanges and mutual learning among civilizations, Shaanxi established the Shaanxi International Communication Center, an external communication platform with Shaanxi characteristics. Taking the 10th anniversary of the Belt & Road Initiative as an opportunity, the centre has shown the highlights and achievements of Shaanxi in serving the country's opening up to the outside world in an all-round way. It organized a series of press conferences on the 10th anniversary of the Belt & Road Initiative, compiled and published the "Blue Book of Shaanxi Province Promoting the Belt and Road Initiative (2013-2023)". During the 7th Silk Road International Expo, we held an exhibition on the achievements of the 10th anniversary of the "Belt and Road Initiative" and a forum on the high-quality development of the China-Europe Railway Express Xi'an Assembly Center, so as to tell the story of Shaanxi and the Silk Road to the world.

2024年陕西经济社会发展主要目标

Major Social and Economic Goals of Shaanxi Province in 2024

生产总值增长5.5%左右,一般公共预算收入增长3%,城乡居民人均可支配收入分别增长5.5%、6.5%。城镇新增就业40万人以上,城镇调查失业率5.5%左右,居民消费价格涨幅3%左右,粮食产量1260万吨以上。单位生产总值能耗降低2.5%以上,力争"十四五"以来累计降低10%左右。

In 2024, GDP of Shaanxi is expected to grow by 5.5%, with a 3% increase in the general public budget revenue, 5.5% and 6.5% increase in the income of urban and rural residents respectively. Over 400,000 new jobs will be created in urban areas, and the surveyed unemployment rate will be controlled under 5.5% in urban areas. The consumer prices will rise by about 3%.The output of grain is over 12.6 million tons.Energy consumption per unit of GDP will be reduced by over 2.5%, and we will strive to reduce it by about 10% cumulatively since the implementation of the "14th Five-Year Plan".

榆林光伏发电推动高质量发展

天下黄河一壶收
——壶口瀑布
The Magnificent Scenery of the Yellow River: Hukou Waterfall

黄色波涛汹涌，河水轰隆作响，白雾在深谷中蒸腾，天边挂起一道彩虹……

这就是"天下黄河一壶收"的黄河壶口瀑布。

黄河壶口瀑布声如雷鸣，气势壮观，是世界上最大的黄色瀑布，也是伟大的中华民族的象征。

黄河壶口瀑布是一条金黄色干流大瀑布，也是移动式、潜伏式大瀑布。黄河流经秦晋峡谷宜川段，滔滔黄河水从千米河床排山倒海似的涌来，骤然归于二三十米宽的"龙槽"，倾注如壶口，形成极为壮观的瀑布群。壶口瀑布四季景色各异，八大自然景观各具特色，波涛汹涌激荡民族之音，勇往直前彰显中华气节，素被国人誉为"黄河之心、民族之魂"。如今这里已形成以壶口瀑布为核心、秦晋峡谷为主体，集瀑布、峡谷、龙王辿、

The tumultuous Yellow River rumbles ahead, and white mist steams in the deep valley with a rainbow hanging in the sky.

This is Hukou Waterfall--the magnificent scenery of the Yellow River.

As the largest yellow waterfall in the world, the thundering Hukou Waterfall of the Yellow River is rolling forward with a magnificent spectacle, symbolizing the great Chinese nation

Hukou Waterfall of the Yellow River is a golden mainstream waterfall,and a mobile, submerged one as well. When the Yellow River runs through the Yichuan section of the Qinjin Canyon, the turbid torrents surge forward with irresistible force from thousand-meter riverbed, and suddenly gather in a twenty-to-thirty-meter- wide "dragon trough", like being poured out from the mouth of the pot, which forms an spectacular waterfall group. The scenery of Hukou Waterfall bears distinctive charm in four seasons, and the eight natural landscapes possess unique features of their own. The mighty river is roaring to the tune of Chinese nation's song, marching forward with the courageous Chinese spirit. Therefore, Hukou Waterfall is reputed as "the heart of the Yellow River and the soul

十里龙槽、孟门山、大禹庙、古渡口小镇、黄河大合唱实景演出等为一体的文化旅游景区。

黄河是中华民族的母亲河，壶口瀑布则是中华民族自强不息、百折不挠的精神象征。1938年9月，抗日战争进入最艰苦的时期，著名诗人光未然带领抗敌演出队来到壶口，在这里，他写下了不朽的诗篇《黄河颂》。回到延安，冼星海为这首诗谱了曲，奏响时代最强音的《黄河大合唱》就此诞生。

"君不见黄河之水天上来，奔流到海不复回"，气势磅礴的壶口瀑布，以其深广的精神内涵，吸引着炎黄子孙，凝聚着中华民族的"民族魂"。

of the nation". Today a cultural tourism scenic spot has been formed with Hukou Waterfall as the core and Qinjin Canyon as the main body, integrating waterfalls, canyons, Ruins of Longwangchan, Ten-Li Dragon Trough, Mengmen Mountain, Dayu Temple, ancient ferry town and live performance of Yellow River Chorus.

The Yellow River is the mother river of the Chinese nation, and Hukou Waterfall represents Chinese spirit of self-improvement and unyielding determination. In September 1938 when the War of Resistance Against Japanese Aggression experienced the toughest period, Guang Weiran, the famous poet, led the anti-Japanese troupe to Hukou, where he wrote the poem "Ode to the Yellow River". Back in Yan'an, Xian Xinghai composed the music for the poem, called "the Yellow River Cantata", playing the strongest sound of the time.

"Do you not see the Yellow River come from the sky, rushing into the sea and never come back?" Representing a profound spiritual connotation, the majestic Hukou Waterfall has attracted all Chinese people and epitomized the national soul.

黄河壶口瀑布

富平县曹村镇太白村华丽柿子合作社群众在制作柿饼

Annex

附录

附录一
三秦城市概览

Annex I
Overview of Major Cities in Shaanxi Province

千年古都　常来长安
Xi'an, a city of thousands of years of history, is welcoming friends near and afar

西安古称长安，是陕西省省会、世界历史文化名城，国家重要的科研、教育和工业基地。作为古丝绸之路的起点，西安正在向亚欧合作交流的国际化大都市迈进。

Xi'an, known as Chang'an in ancient times, is the capital of Shaanxi, a famous historical and cultural city in the world, an important base for science, education and industries of China. As the starting point of ancient Silk Road, Xi'an is developing to be an international metropolis for Eurasian cooperation and exchanges.

青铜之乡　文明宝鸡
Baoji, hometown of bronze ware with brilliant civilization

宝鸡古称陈仓，是陕西省第二大城市，也是我国承接东西、连通南北的重要交通枢纽。宝鸡是我国西部工业重镇，有"中国钛谷"之称。

Baoji, known as Chencang in ancient times, is the second largest city of Shaanxi and an important traffic hub linking the east with the west, and the north with the south. Baoji is also an important industrial city in western China. It is also known as the "Titanium Valley of China".

大秦故都 德善咸阳
Xianyang, capital of the Qin Dynasty and land of virtue

咸阳是中华民族繁荣富强的发端地和秦文化的发源地，也是中国大地原点所在地、中国农耕文明的发祥地。咸阳现已发展成为国家重要的商品粮生产基地和优质苹果、蔬菜生产基地。

Xianyang is the cradle of prosperous and powerful China and a source of the Qin civilization. It is the geodetic origin of China. It has a sound agricultural basis and is the birthplace of China's farming civilization. Today, Xianyang is an important base for commodity grain, high-quality apples and vegetables in China.

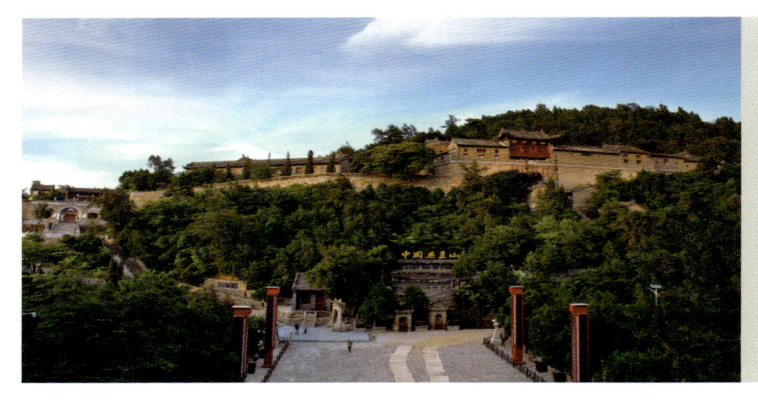

药王故里 五彩铜川
Tongchuan, beautiful hometown of Herb King

铜川是药王孙思邈故里，也是中国红色革命的根据地、黑色煤炭的富集地和绿色生态的养生地。耀州窑久负盛名，中国历史文化名镇陈炉被誉为"东方古陶瓷生产活化石"。

Tongchuan is the home town of Herb King Sun Simiao. It is also a revolutionary base, a place with plentiful coal and an ecological land for regimen. Yaozhou Kiln has enjoyed a high reputation for a long time. Chenlu, a famous Chinese historical and cultural town, is honored as a "living fossil for oriental ancient ceramics production".

三圣故里 人文渭南
Weinan, the Home of Three Saints with humanity

渭南是中华民族的重要发祥地，是中国的戏曲之乡和民俗之乡。渭南工农业齐头并进，既被称为陕西的"粮仓""棉库"，也有"中国钼都""华夏金城"之誉。

Weinan is an important cradle of the Chinese nation and also known as a hometown for operas and folk customs. Both industry and agriculture are well-developed in Weinan. As the "Granary" and "Cotton Warehouse" of Shaanxi, Weinan also has the titles of "capital of molybdenum" and "gold city" of China for its plentiful mineral resources.

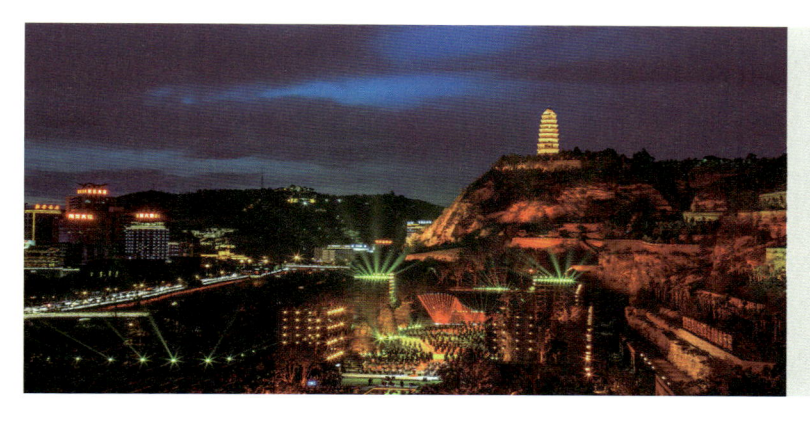

革命圣地 魅力延安
Yan'an, a charming and holy revolutionary land

延安是历史文化名城，全国优秀旅游城市和爱国主义、革命传统、延安精神三大教育基地。延安旅游资源独具特色，旅游业具有广阔前景；矿产资源丰富，是中国石油工业的发祥地。

Yan'an is one of famous historical and cultural cities, national excellent tourism cities, and an education base for patriotism, revolutionary tradition and the Yan'an spirit. Yan'an has unique cultural tourism resources and great potential in tourism. Yan'an boasts abundant mineral resources. It is the cradle land of China's petroleum industry.

能源新都　幸福榆林
Yulin, new capital of energy and great place for a happy life

榆林素有"九边重镇"之美誉，是国家历史文化名城。榆林自古多元文化交汇，集边塞、游牧、黄土、红色文化于一体。榆林能源富集，是建设中的国家能源化工基地。

Yulin has been known as a "key frontier city". As one of famous historical and cultural cities, Yulin has been a hub of diverse cultures, such as frontier culture, nomadic culture, loess culture and revolutionary culture, since ancient times. Boasting rich mineral resources, Yulin is a national energy and chemical base under construction.

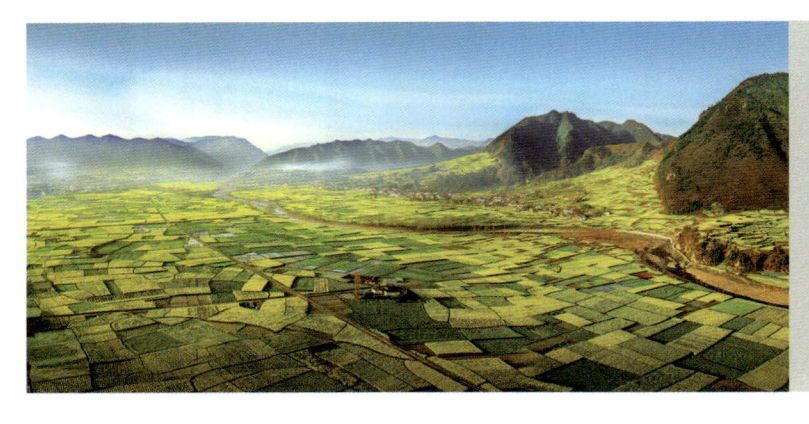

两汉三国　真美汉中
Hanzhong, a beautiful land known for the Han Dynasty and Three Kingdom's Culture

汉中是国家历史文化名城，两汉三国文化的主要发祥地，名列"中国最美十大城镇"。汉中生物资源丰富，素有"生物资源宝库"之称，也是全国重要的中药材生产基地。

Hanzhong is one of famous historical and cultural cities and the main birthplace of the the Han Dynasty and Three Kingdoms' Culture. It is one of "China's Top 10 Beautiful Cities". Hanzhong is rich in biological resources and enjoys the reputation of "biological resource treasure". It is also an important herb production base in China.

秦巴明珠 生态安康
Ankang, an ecological city like a pearl in Qin-Ba hinterland

安康是我国西部地区重要的清洁能源基地、区域交通枢纽，也是"南水北调"中线工程核心水源区。安康自然资源富集，是全国富硒茶、绞股蓝、魔芋之乡。

Ankang is an important clean energy base and a regional traffic hub in western China. It is also the core water source zone for the middle route of the national "South-to-North Water Diversion Project". Ankang boasts rich natural resources and is the home of selenium-enriched tea, Gynostemma Pentaphyllum and konjac.

雄秦秀楚 最美商洛
Shangluo, a charming city with the Qin's majesty and Chu's beauty

商洛地跨长江、黄河两大流域，为革命老区，有丰富的生物、矿产和旅游资源。现已形成现代材料、现代中药、绿色食品、生态旅游四大特色产业体系。

Straddling the basins of the Yangtze River and the Yellow River, Shangluo is an old revolutionary base and has rich biological, mineral and tourism resources. Today, the city has formed four major specialty industrial systems, namely, modern materials, modern herbs, green food and ecological tourism.

附录二
2016 年以来，
陕西入选"全国十大考古新发现"的考古遗址

Annex II
Shaanxi's Archaeological Sites Listed on China's Annual Top 10 Archaeological Sites Discovered since 2016

2016 年　陕西凤翔雍山血池秦汉祭祀遗址
Yongshan Xuechi Sacrifice Site of the Qin and Han Dynasties, Fengxiang, Shaanxi, 2016

该遗址为首次在秦都雍城附近发现的与古文献记载相吻合，时代较早、规模最大、性质明确、持续时间最长，且功能结构趋于完整的国家大型祭祀遗址。

It is the first sacrifice site discovered near Yongcheng, the capital of Qin Kingdom, and complies with ancient records. It features early history, big scale, definite nature, long existence and completeness in function and structure as a large-scale national sacrifice site.

2017 年　陕西高陵杨官寨遗址
Yangguanzhai Site, Gaoling, Shaanxi, 2017

墓葬年代为庙底沟文化时期，是国内首次确认的庙底沟文化大型成人墓地。

The site is a large-sized adult tomb of the Miaodigou Civilization Period confirmed for the first time in China.

2017年 陕西西安秦汉栎阳城遗址
The Yueyang City Site of Qin and Han Dynasties, Xi'an, Shaanxi, 2017

遗址内首次出土了清晰的"栎阳"陶文，确认了"商鞅变法"发生地正是栎阳。栎阳城是中国城市发展阶段上的重要环节，对研究秦汉都城的规划、中国城市的发展史都有重要价值。

Pottery inscribed with clear characters "Yueyang" were first unearthed at the site, proving "Shang Yang's Reform" took place in Yueyang. As an important step in China's city development, Yueyang City is of great value to study the capital planning of the Qin and Han dynasties as well as the evolution history of China's cities.

2018年 陕西延安芦山峁新石器时代遗址
Lushanmao Neolithic Site, Yan'an, Shaanxi, 2018

该遗址以四座台城式建筑群为核心，面积超过200万平方米。四座台城中最大的"大营盘梁"部分分布着三座院落，由北部一座大型院落和南部两座小型院落构成"品"字形布局。

The site is centered on four Taicheng-style buildings, covering an area of more than 2 million square meters. The largest of the four Taicheng "Da Ying Pan Liang" department is distributed with three courtyards—a large courtyard in the north and two small courtyards in the south, forming a layout of the Chinese character "pin".

2018 年　陕西澄城刘家洼东周遗址
Liujiawa Site of the Eastern Zhou Dynasty, Chengcheng, Shaanxi, 2018

遗址由城址、居址和墓地组成，发掘清理出大量青铜器以及金器、玉器、铁器、陶器和漆木器等珍贵文物。推断这里是芮国后期的都城遗址及墓地，该遗址的发现填补了芮国后期历史的空白。

The site, composed of the city part, the residence part and the base of the city, was excavated a large number of valuable cultural relics like bronze, gold, jade, iron, pottery and lacquered wood artifacts. It is inferred that this is the capital city site and cemetery in later period of Ruiguo (one of vassal states during the Western Zhou Dynasty and the Spring and Autumn Period), which fills the gap in the history of this period. The discovery of the site has filled a gap in the history of late Rui.

2019 年　陕西神木石峁遗址皇城台
The Imperial Platform of Shimao Site, Shenmu, Shaanxi, 2019

石峁遗址皇城台是内城和外城重重拱卫的核心，或已具备早期"宫城"性质，是目前东亚地区保存最好、规模最大的早期宫城建筑，展现了黄土高原上一处神秘王国都邑的极致辉煌。

Surrounded and protected by the inner and outer cities, the Imperial Platform of Shimao Site may have already functioned as an early imperial city. It is the best preserved and the largest early palace complex in East Asia, showing the ultimate glory of the mysterious kingdom capital on the Loess Plateau.

2020 年　陕西西安少陵原十六国大墓
Sixteen Kingdoms Tombs in Shaolingyuan Plateau, Xi'an，Shaanxi, 2020

遗址有三座规格巨大、形制特殊、结构完整的十六国时期高等级墓葬，出土土雕建筑、壁画以及彩绘陶俑等，是国内迄今为止发现的规模最大的十六国时期高等级墓葬。

Three high-level tombs of the Sixteen Kingdoms Period were excavated with huge size, peculiar shape and complete structure, along with earth sculpture architecture, murals and painted pottery figurines. They are the largest high-level tombs of the Sixteen Kingdoms Period discovered in China up to now.

2021年 陕西西安江村大墓
Jiangcun Village Tomb, Xi'an, Shaanxi, 2021

遗址的发掘确定了霸陵的准确位置，解决了西汉十一陵的名位问题。为西汉帝陵制度形成、发展、演变的研究提供了翔实的考古资料，为中国古代帝王陵墓制度的深入研究奠定了基础。

The excavation of Jiangcun Village Tomb helped to determine the exact location of the Ba Mausoleum and solved the problem of the name and position of 11 mausoleums of the Western Han Dynasty. In addition, the excavation has provided detailed archaeological data for the study of the formation, development and evolution of the imperial mausoleum system in the Western Han Dynasty, and laid foundation for the in-depth study of the imperial mausoleum system in ancient China.

2022年 陕西旬邑西头遗址
Xitou Ruins, Xunyi, Shaanxi Province, 2022

该遗址是目前泾河流域考古发现规模最大、等级最高的商周时期遗址。发掘出了西周时期的大型城址，及10余座西周时期甲字形大墓，构建起区域商周时期的年代序列，为寻找文献所记载西周"豳师"提供了重要线索。

So far, Xitou Ruins ranks the largest and highest standard of the Shang and Zhou period discovered in the Jinghe River basin. Unearthed were a large city site of the Western Zhou Dynasty and more than 10 large tombs of the Shang and Zhou period in the shape of the nail. These discoveries build up a chronological sequence of the Shang and Zhou period and provide important clues to the search for the "Binshi(an ancient city)" of the Western Zhou Dynasty recorded in history.

2023年 陕西清涧寨沟遗址
Zhaigou Ruins, Qingjian, Shaanxi Province, 2023

寨沟遗址是近年来商代方国考古的重大突破，出土的金耳环、蛇首匕、陶器具有鲜明的地方特色，反映了黄土丘陵地区与商王朝之间密切的经济、文化交流，以及商王朝对周边地区的强烈影响。

Zhaigou Ruins, Qingjian County, Shaanxi Province in 2023 Zhaigou Ruins represents a significant archaeological breakthrough of the tribal states in the Shang Dynasty in recently years. The gold earrings, snakehead-shaped daggers, and potteries unearthed from Zhaigou Ruins are characterized with distinctive local features, reflecting the frequent economic and cultural exchanges between states in the Loess Hills areas and the Shang Dynasty, and Shang Dynasty's strong influence on the neighboring regions.

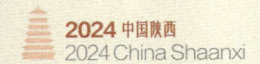

附录三
巧夺天工的陕西国宝级文物

Annex III
Shaanxi Cultural Relics with Exquisite Workmanship

秦始皇帝陵博物院 铜车马
Emperor Qinshihuang's Mausoleum Site,
Copper Carriages of Emperor

陕西历史博物馆 兽首玛瑙杯
Shaanxi History Museum,
Beast Head-shaped
Agate Cup

宝鸡青铜器博物院 西周墙盘
Baoji Bronze Ware Museum,
Western Zhou's Qiang Basin

法门寺博物馆 铜浮屠
Famen Temple Museum,
Copper Pagoda

法门寺博物馆 八重宝函
Famen Temple Museum,
Eight Cases

西安碑林博物馆　景云铜钟
Xi'an Beilin Museum,
Jingyun Bronze Bell

西安碑林博物馆　大秦景教流行中国碑
Xi'an Beilin Museum,
Stele on Nestorianism from Eastern
Roman Empire's Spread in China

宝鸡青铜器博物院　何尊
Baoji Bronze Museum,
HeZun

陕西历史博物馆　淳化大鼎
Shaanxi History Museum,
Chunhua Caldron

法门寺博物馆　银花双轮十二环锡杖
Famen Temple Museum,
A Monk's Cane with Silver Flowers
and 12 Rings

陕西茂陵博物馆　茂陵石雕
Shaanxi Maoling Mausoleum
Museum,
Stone Sculpture of Mausoleum
Museum

陕西历史博物馆　舞马衔杯仿皮囊式银壶
Shaanxi History Museum,
Leather Bag-shaped Silver Pot with
a Dancing Horse Holding a Cup in
Its Mouth

附录四
陕西第一批"国家级非物质文化遗产"名录

Annex IV
The First Batch of "National Intangible Cultural Heritage" in Shaanxi

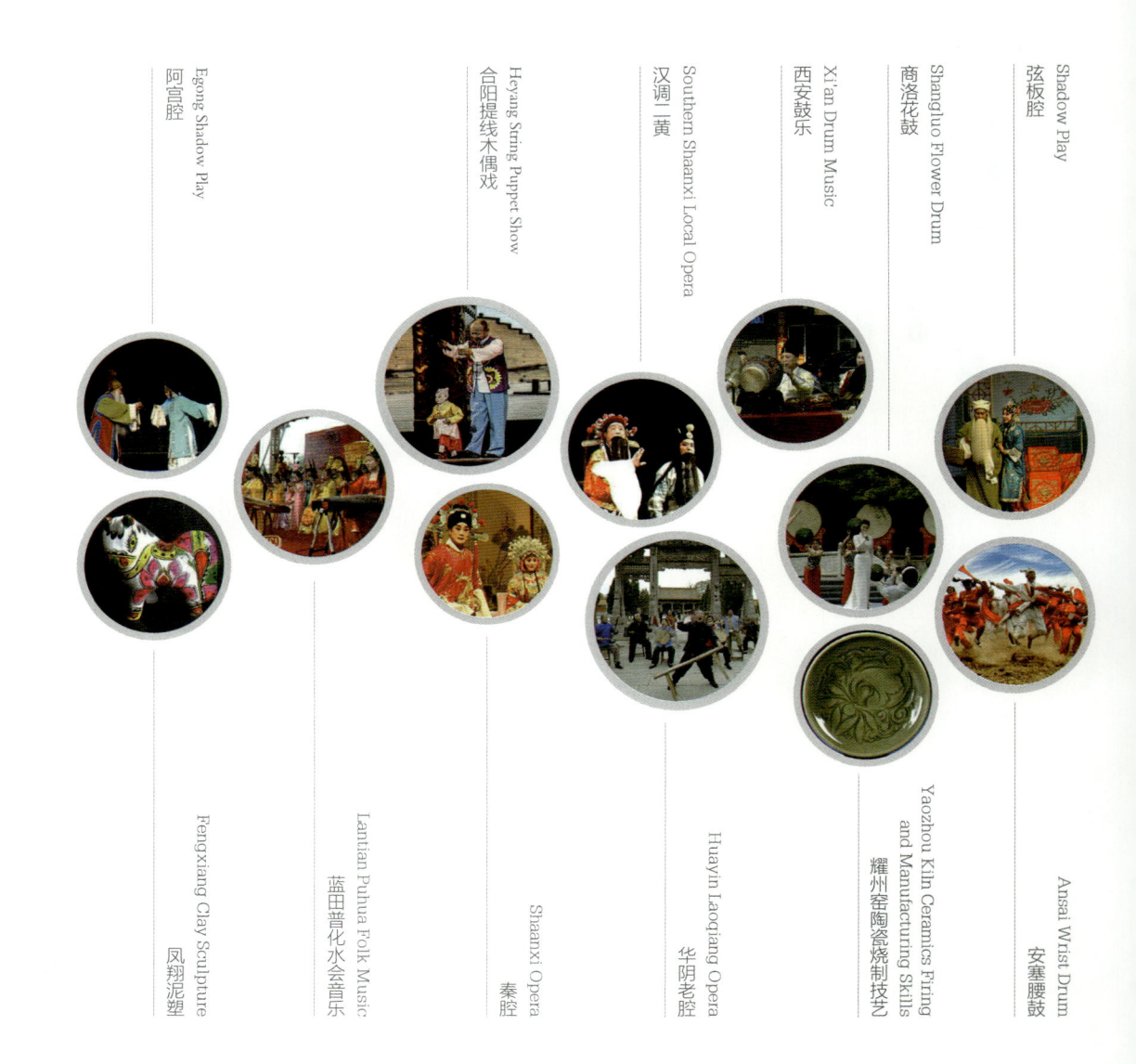

- 弦板腔 Shadow Play
- 商洛花鼓 Shangluo Flower Drum
- 西安鼓乐 Xi'an Drum Music
- 汉调二黄 Southern Shaanxi Local Opera
- 合阳提线木偶戏 Heyang String Puppet Show
- 阿宫腔 Egong Shadow Play
- 凤翔泥塑 Fengxiang Clay Sculpture
- 蓝田普化水会音乐 Lantian Puhua Folk Music
- 秦腔 Shaanxi Opera
- 华阴老腔 Huayin Laoqiang Opera
- 耀州窑陶瓷烧制技艺 Yaozhou Kiln Ceramics Firing and Manufacturing Skills
- 安塞腰鼓 Ansai Wrist Drum

Northern Shaanxi Yangge Performance
陕北秧歌

Ziyang Folk Song
紫阳民歌

Sacrificial Rites at the Mausoleum of the Yellow Emperor
黄帝陵祭典

Ansai Paper cutting
安塞剪纸

Huaxian County shadow Puppet
华县皮影戏

Hanzhong Local Opera
汉调桄桄

Northern Shaanxi Storytelling
陕北说书

Fengxiang Xylograph New Year Pictures
凤翔木版年画

Chengcheng Yaotou Ceramics Firing and Manufacturing Skills
澄城尧头陶瓷烧制技艺

Luochuan Bouncing Drum Dance (Biegu)
洛川蹩鼓

Yulin Folk Tune
榆林小曲

Baoji Shehuo
宝鸡社火

141

附录五
陕西特产

Annex V
Shaanxi Specialties

临潼石榴
Lintong Pomegranate

石榴相传为西汉张骞出使西域时引进的，距今已有2000多年的历史。临潼石榴皮红个儿大，皮薄籽满，色泽鲜艳，味美可口。

Lintong Pomegranate, having a history of more than 2,000 years, features a thin and red peel, large size, bright color and delicious taste. It is said that pomegranate was introduced to China when Zhang Qian visited the western countries along the Silk Road in the Han Dynasty.

西凤酒
Xifeng Liquor

西凤酒产于宝鸡市凤翔区，因凤翔位于关中西部，故称西凤酒。西凤酒距今已有2600多年的历史，是我国八大名酒之一，远销海内外。

Xifeng Liquor is produced in Fengxiang, a county to the west of Guanzhong. With a history of more than 2,600 years, the liquor is one of China's eight famous liquors and widely sold across the world.

陕北红枣
Northern Shaanxi Red Date

陕北红枣主要产于黄河沿岸的宜川、延川、清涧、吴堡、佳县、神木、府谷等地，它以果大、核小、皮薄、肉厚、味醇、油性大、色红、酸甜可口，含丰富的蛋白质、维生素、矿物质闻名于世。

Northern Shaanxi Red Dates, mainly produced in Yichuan, Yanchuan, Qingjian, Wubu, Jiaxian, Shenmu, Fugu and other counties along the Yellow River, are world-famous due to the big size, small core, thin peel, thick pulp, pure flavor, high oil content, red color, nice taste, and rich content of protein, vitamin and mineral.

稠酒
Choujiu Wine

稠酒又名"黄桂稠酒",是一种古老名酒,盛唐时期朝野上下无不饮之。党和国家领导人多次用它来招待和宴请贵宾。郭沫若曾称赞它"不像酒,胜似酒"。

Choujiu Wine, a famous ancient wine also known as "Huanggui Choujiu Wine", was quite popular in the Tang Dynasty. Leaders entertained domestic and foreign guests with the wine. "It doesn't taste like wine, but its taste is better than wine" was Guo Moruo's praise for the wine.

陕南茶叶
Southern Shaanxi Tea

陕茶主要种植区域在巴山北麓陕南三市所辖的28个县(区)。著名品牌有汉中仙毫、紫阳富硒茶、商南泉茗、定军茗眉、汉水银梭、午子仙毫,以及用陕南茶叶制作的黑茶系列——泾渭茯茶等。

The north slope of the Bashan Mountain, 28 counties and districts under the jurisdiction of three Southern Shaanxi cities are the main tea planting areas of Shaanxi.

The famous tea brands include Hanzhong Xianhao, Ziyang Se-enriched Tea, Shangnan Quanming, Dingjun Mingmei, Hanshui Yinsuo and Wuzi Xianhao, and the black tea Jingwei Fu Tea made of southern Shaanxi tea leaves.

核桃
Walnut

陕西渭北一带和商洛地区是著名的核桃之乡,年产量为全国第一。核桃富含蛋白质、维生素、矿物质,对人体有较强的保健作用。

The northern region of the Weihe River and the Shangluo prefecture are the famous producing areas of walnuts and rank China's No. 1 in annual yield. Walnuts are healthy because of their high content of protein, vitamins and minerals.

苹果
Apple

陕西苹果是全球知名品牌，已经被定为国礼，产量、品质均为中国第一。因为陕西的渭北平原和黄土高原地带日照充足，昼夜温差适当，最适宜苹果生长，故陕西苹果酥脆香甜，微酸爽口，汁多味正。

Shaanxi Apples, a world-famous brand, are honored as a national gift thanks to their supreme production and quality in China. The Weibei Plain and Loess Plateau of Shaanxi are the most appropriate regions for growing apple trees thanks to the sufficient sunshine and moderate diurnal amplitude. Thus, the apples are sweet, crisp, dainty, juicy and flavorful.

中华猕猴桃
Actinidia Chinensis

中华猕猴桃小的似核桃，大的如鹅卵，皮色褐绿，内瓤翠绿，清香酸甜，营养价值较高。它除了可以食鲜果外，还可加工成果汁、果酒和果酱等。

Actinidia Chinensis (Chinese kiwi fruit), is the size of walnuts or goose eggs. With breen peel and green pulp, the fragrant and sweet fruit has high nutrition value. It can also be processed into juice, wine and jam.

临潼火晶柿子
Lintong Fire Crystal Persimmon

火晶柿子是临潼特有的柿树品种。柿子个儿小色红，晶莹光亮，皮薄无核，深受国内外游客喜爱。

Lintong Fire Crystal Persimmon, a unique persimmon in Lintong featuring small size, red color, bright appearance, thin peel and small core, is greatly favored by domestic and foreign guests.

富平柿饼
Fuping Dried Persimmon

富平柿饼又称富平合儿饼，以富平县自产的优质柿子制成。形似圆月，肉红透明，无子，凝霜后，白里透红、皮脆柔软、清甜爽口，因两个相对成一合而得名。富平柿饼营养丰富，具有润肺、补血、健胃、止咳等药理功效。

It is also called Fuping Dual Pie and made of high quality persimmon produced in Fuping. It is a round, transparent flesh-colored candied fruit without seeds. The frosty ones are reddish white, crisp in peel and soft in pulp. Two persimmons are placed oppositely in a package, thus called Dual Pie. It is nutritious and has a medicinal effect on lungs, blood and stomach and relieves coughs.

秦椒
Qin Pepper

秦椒素有"椒中之王"的美称，是陕西一项大宗出口商品，畅销国际市场。

Qin Pepper, known as "the king of peppers", is a sort of bulk export of Shaanxi and widely sold in global market.

陕北小米
Northern Shaanxi Millet

陕北小米是指产于陕北延安、榆林一带的小米。陕北地区光热资源充足，昼夜温差大，因而盛产谷子。谷子成熟后稍经加工，即成黄灿灿、香喷喷的小米。得益于得天独厚的自然条件，陕北小米养分积累多，营养价值高，是极具特色的陕西特产。

It refers to the millet produced in Yan'an and Yulin of northern Shaanxi. The sufficient light, heat and temperature difference between day and night contribute to the growth of millet plants. The matured plants become the yellow and sweet millet through simple processing. Thanks to the advantageous natural conditions, the millet absorbs plentiful nutrient and boasts rich nutrition. It is a highly recognizable Shaanxi specialty.

附录六
陕西精华旅游线路

Annex VI
Best Tourist Routes in Shaanxi

1 日游 One-day Tour

线路一 西安古都一日游（市内） Route A: One-day Tour in Ancient Capital Xi'an (Downtown)

钟鼓楼　陕西历史博物馆　碑林　城墙　书院门文化一条街

Bell and Drum Towers—Shaanxi History Museum—Xi'an Stele Forest—Xi'an City Wall—Shuyuanmen Cultural Street

线路二 西安古都一日游（市内） Route B: One-day Tour in Ancient Capital Xi'an (Downtown)

大雁塔　大唐芙蓉园　小雁塔　清真大寺　高家大院　坊上清真小吃一条街

Giant Wild Goose Pagoda—Tang Paradise—Small Wild Goose Pagoda—Great Mosque—Courtyard of Family Gao—Fangshang Muslim Snack Street

线路三 东线一日游 Route C: One-day Eastward Tour

秦始皇帝陵博物院　华清池　秦始皇陵　半坡博物馆

Emperor Qinshihuang's Mausoleum site—Huaqing Pool—Mausoleum of Emperor Qinshihuang—Banpo Museum

线路四 西岳华山一日游 Route D: One-day Tour to Huashan Mountain

线路五 西线一日游 Route E: One-day Westward Tour

法门寺　乾陵　永泰公主墓

Famen Temple—Qianling Mausoleum—Princess Yongtai's Tomb

2日游 Two-day Tour

线路一 东线二日游 Route A: Two-day Eastward Tour

第一日 D1

西安—华山—韩城

Xi'an—Huashan Mountain—Hancheng

第二日 D2

党家村—司马迁祠—韩城文庙—黄河龙门—西安

Dangjia Village—Sima Qian Temple—Confucius Temple in Hancheng—Longmen of the Yellow River—Xi'an

线路二 西线二日游 Route B: Two-day Westward Tour

第一日 D1

西安—乾陵—法门寺—宝鸡

Xi'an—Qianling Mausoleum—Famen Temple—Baoji

第二日 D2

宝鸡青铜器博物院—楼观台—西安

Baoji Bronze Ware Museum—Louguantai Temple—Xi'an

附录七
陕西小吃

Annex VII
Shaanxi Snacks

灌汤包子
Steamed Stuffed Bun with Soup

粉蒸肉
Steamed Pork with Rice Flour

麻酱凉皮
Cold Rice Noodles with Sesame Sauce

羊肉泡馍
Pita Bread Soaked in Lamb Soup

肉丸胡辣汤
Meatballs in Pepper and Spicy Soup

乾县豆腐脑
Jellied Bean Curd of Qianxian County

金线油塔
Crispy Fried Noodles

酸汤水饺
Dumplings in Sour Soup

大米凉皮
Cold Rice Noodles

腊汁肉夹馍
Rougamo

邋遢面
Shaanxi Handmade Noodles

甑糕
Glutinous Rice and Date Cake

149

荞面饸饹
Buckwheat Vermicelli

擀面皮
Rolled Cold Steamed Noodles

水盆羊肉
Mutton in Water Basin

锅盔辣子
Flour Pancake with Green Pepper

臊子面
Minced Pork Noodles

柿子饼
Dried Persimmon

豆花泡馍
Steamed Bun with Bean Curd

黄米糕
Yellow Rice Cake

洋芋擦擦
Steamed Potato Slices

黄馍馍
Yellow Steamed Bun

菜豆腐
Vegetarian Tofu

炕炕馍
Sesame Seed Cake

热米皮
Hot Rice Noodles

图书在版编目（CIP）数据

2024中国陕西/陕西省人民政府新闻办公室编. —西安：陕西人民出版社, 2024.4

ISBN 978-7-224-15343-9

Ⅰ.①2… Ⅱ.①陕… Ⅲ.①陕西—概况 Ⅳ.①K924.1

中国国家版本馆CIP数据核字（2024）第062722号

责任编辑 | 韩　琳
　　　　　　王　倩
　　　　　　武晓雨
翻　　译 | 杨冬敏
　　　　　　徐闻蔚
英文审校 | 张　敏

2024中国陕西
2024 ZHONGGUO SHAANXI

编　　者　陕西省人民政府新闻办公室
出版发行　陕西人民出版社
　　　　　（西安市北大街147号　邮编：710003）
印　　刷　陕西金和印务有限公司
开　　本　787mm×1092mm　1/16
印　　张　10.5
字　　数　150千字
版　　次　2024年4月第1版
印　　次　2024年4月第1次印刷
书　　号　ISBN 978-7-224-15343-9
定　　价　68.00元

如有印装质量问题，请与本社联系调换。电话：029-87205094